A reporter's look at the people and events
that made Memphis what it is today.

MEMPHIS

The South Unscripted

John Branston

For Jenny, Jack and Katy

Foreword

Come Let Us Praise Infamous Men

by Henry Turley

Whenever my old buddies get together, we don't have to add much whiskey before someone recounts a Tiller story. It's usually rendered apocryphal by the insertion of too many "I's", but no one cares; the teller isn't really central, it's all about George, or Mike, or Dago.

Thus prompted we offer tales of Canales — Adonis Whit and Gargantuan Justin. Maybe a joke about Bill Tanner's willingness to do our yard work — at least the tree trimming. And if anyone's serious enough to talk politics it's "can you believe what Willie or Harold did today?" Followed by a "Well, if Mr. Crump were still here . . . ." and "thank God Freddie Smith is".

Without really understanding what we're doing or why, we chant through the mythology of Memphis, of outsized heroes, where the protagonists and antagonists are ambiguous and easily confused.

And while the names can change over the generations — all the way back to Mike Fink and Davy Crockett and General Jackson — the stories remain the same because it's these tales that form us. Their endless retelling lets us not know but somehow sense who we are and enables us to slip our lives quietly into roles where we too add imperceptibly to the ineluctable flow of our history.

Our heroes are at times outlaws and always outsized. They're defined by their reckless energy, fire, determination and always their freedom and willful independence. Their stories are played out at the headwaters of the great river delta in a sprawling half-city that was ripped from the immemorial wilderness 175 years ago in a grand real estate scheme that is still being contested.

I've always supposed that Mr. Crump was the great aberration summonsed by our essential anarchy. He was to try to repress and structure us into some momentary order. But Willie Herenton is our living, ruling personification, the inscrutable titan astride our elemental tempest.

History in Nashville, as in most cities, derives methodically from consensus. In Memphis, history is just a statistical average — normalizing the deeds of mad men — and it's made at the edges.

Reporters like to call their work "the first rough draft of history." Sometimes it is best left told that way — atomistic, anarchic, raw, and in morsels that stimulate our appetites — at least that's so in Memphis.

We, who have been told by Faulkner that our past is not dead and not even past, are living our history now in bits so discrete as to be incomprehensible. Our tales play out before the watchful eye of John Branston, who, for one reason or another, is a simple seeker of truths.

(Henry Turley is a lifelong Memphian who develops real estate, mostly in Memphis' downtown and inner city.)

Table of Contents

Introduction

"All the rowdiness of Memphis endears it to me."
– author Shelby Foote in a 1996 interview
for *Memphis* magazine.

This is a book about Memphis and the South, but there is almost nothing in it about Elvis, barbecue, the blues, Baptists, the mighty Mississippi River, or anyone's mama or granny. In 25 years as a reporter in Tennessee and Mississippi, I have written about those things but many others have done it much better. The people and stories that interested me the most were developers, businessmen, writers, gamblers, prosecutors, and politicians who were rough cut, candid, and willing to spend time with me. If they were not always fun to be around when things did not go well, that is often the nature of news. John Grisham didn't make these stories up. This is Memphis unscripted.

It's only journalism. Nobody knows that better than me. But it is true, or most of it is as far as I can tell anyway. In March of 1979, I drove a Volkswagen from Wisconsin to Nashville in search of work, was turned down for jobs at the two daily papers, and before heading for Huntsville, Birmingham and Atlanta decided to call the UPI bureau just in case. The bureau chief, Duren Cheek, hired me over the phone as a summer replacement, and I have been a reporter in Nashville, Jackson, Mississippi, and Memphis ever since at UPI, *The*

Commercial Appeal, Memphis magazine, *The Memphis Flyer*, as well as a freelancer.

I've never been an editor or desk man. My only venture into advertising was a three-word slogan: Midtown Is Memphis. I didn't make any money on the bumper sticker, which says something about my business acumen. Besides that, I have written close to two million words about Memphis, Mississippi, Arkansas, and Tennessee. Most of it was old news the day after it was printed. But even after as long as 20 years, a few stories still seem to me worth updating and revisiting for several reasons.

Memphis history since the Martin Luther King Jr. assassination is often written by academics citing journalists as part of their research. Newspaper reporters and editors come and go. By necessity news stories, my own included, often rely on Internet archives, today's version of the newsroom morgue. As a freelancer for national newspapers and television and movie producers, I have done legwork for other reporters on Mid-South stories. I'm always impressed with their talent — and their instant omniscience. In this book, I propose to eliminate the middleman. My friend Ken Neill, the publisher of *Memphis* magazine and *The Memphis Flyer*, calls this journalistic turf-protection "peeing on the fire hydrant."

With a few exceptions, there are no second-hand sources in these stories. The interviewing and reporting, for better or worse, were my own. When I wrote about something that happened before I came to Memphis — the death of E. H. "Boss" Crump in 1954, for example — I checked my research with eyewitnesses whenever possible. I have updated some numbers in these stories, edited them for length, and changed tense from present to past when it seemed to make for greater clarity. If a story was revisited several years later, I combined some old and new material but left the quotes and reporting alone. There is a healthy tension in writing about people when they are alive and kicking and, if they are going through bad times, can bite back by picking up the phone or knocking on your door. Too much rewriting can cheat the reader.

Long stories are out of fashion in local and regional journalism. The trend is toward short and snappy. Sports dominate the daily papers, where the latest innovation is encouraging readers to send in their own snapshots and stories for publication. News-you-can-use, home-and-garden features, and glamour photos are the staples of city magazines. Coffee-table books about cities tend to be long on flattering cliches and pretty pictures and short on truth. I've been lucky to work for editors and publishers who believed in reporting without restraint and in-depth stories.

"Mid-South" was *The Commercial Appeal's* staff-produced Sunday magazine, replaced by "Parade" in 1987. From 1983 to 1986, I was allowed weeks, months, and in a couple of cases more than a year to work on a single story. I wish to thank editor Chris Peck for permission to reprint some of them. As a regular contributor to *Memphis* from 1993 until 2000, I was given a free hand and unfailing support by Ken Neill. Long deadlines allow a reporter to roam far and wide, get close to a subject, collect face-to-face quotes and impressions in good and bad times, review the work of other reporters, cultivate sources, and rewrite second, third, and fourth drafts. *The Memphis Flyer* has given me the same privilege for 12 years. A former colleague at *The Commercial Appeal* recently wrote me a note with a condescending reference to my decision to write for "a tabloid." He could not be more wrong. The freedom to experiment, reinvent yourself, and test journalistic rules is the key to survival for both reporters and newspapers, as even the smarter dailies are discovering.

The downside of living in the same city for 22 years is you can get stale and not get much notice outside of Memphis. But as long as people keep talking to you — and that is always a risk — you can become something of an expert about certain things, if only by longevity. As Woody Allen said, 90 percent of life is showing up. Several of the people and events in these stories got national media attention after I and other Memphis reporters wrote about them. Others continue to make news or thrive on the Internet, where the proverbial 15 minutes of fame can become eternal life.

It's funny the things you remember about 25 years in journalism. Several years ago, I was searching for a feature story on a slow day and drove halfway to Corinth, Mississippi, to meet an author named Thomas Hal Phillips. In the early Fifties he had written three novels and some short stories that had received favorable reviews. So favorable, in fact, that the reviewer for *Time* magazine had compared him to

William Faulkner. For a young Mississippi writer to be compared to Faulkner must be the literary equivalent of Irwin Shaw's short story *The 80-yard Run* about a man who never got over his moment of fame on the football field.

We met in a booth of a truckstop restaurant. Thomas Hal Phillips, the prototype for Hal Phillip Walker in the Robert Altman movie "Nashville," was alone, dressed in slacks and a short-sleeved shirt, shy, and polite. All I knew about him was that he was a graduate of Mississippi State and had written some books back when that had won him some notice. What I remember about the interview was his saying that if you read something you wrote a long time ago and it still seems good, then maybe it is, and nobody can take that away from you.

After so many years, some of these stories seem less important, although no less interesting, than they did when I wrote them. Several of them, though, seem more significant in light of events that followed. Radical tax protester Gordon Kahl, shot to death and burned up in a dugout house in the Arkansas Ozarks in 1983, was clearly the prototype of domestic terrorists such as Timothy McVeigh. One young Arkansas prosecutor who followed Kahl's case closely was Asa Hutchinson, now Under Secretary of the Department of Homeland Security. And the seeds of Whitewater and the impeachment of Bill Clinton were planted not only in Arkansas and the White House but also in the 1993 trial of Harold Ford and the career of U.S. Attorney Hickman Ewing Jr., who is mentioned eight times in Clinton's book, *My Life*.

The troubled history of the Memphis City Schools begins with the explosive "Plan Z" desegregation plan endorsed by federal Judge Robert McRae in 1973. He isn't a household name, but anyone in local politics can tell you that suburban developer Waymon "Jackie" Welch Jr. has had a huge impact on suburban sprawl and the location of county schools via his real estate prowess and political connections. People who insist that legalized gambling in Memphis is unconstitutional or impossible do not remember the horse racing saga of Charles McVean from 1987 to 1990, three years before Tunica took off. And the conspiracy theories about James Earl Ray and the 1968 assassination of Dr. Martin Luther King owe a lot to the creative license of Ray's ghostwriter, Tupper Saussy, and a discredited hoax implicating the Army and the Green Berets.

Some names are Memphis icons. Tough guy Charles "Dago" Tiller, who died in 2004, is known to an older generation of Memphians for his violence and his wasted talent. The equally rugged Canale brothers took a different road. Brothers Rick and Ron Schilling are synonymous with Splash Casino and the early days of Tunica. And a city that thinks of itself as the cradle of business entrepreneurs has produced men as different as William B. Tanner, irrepressible as ever at the age of 70, and FedEx founder Fred Smith.

In 25 years as a reporter, it was my good luck and pleasure to write about what interests me for as long as I wanted to. I got to meet and observe extraordinary people over the course of events that made Memphis what it is. This is my contribution.

A reporter's look at the people and events
that made Memphis what it is today.

MEMPHIS
The South Unscripted

John Branston

I.
Politicians and Prosecutors

Curtain Raiser:
50 Years after Boss Crump
(2004)

Boss Crump

Edward Hull Crump, or Boss Crump as he was known, was the most powerful man in Memphis for half a century and important enough on the national political scene to make the cover of Time *magazine in 1946. He died in 1954, leaving Memphis a city known as one of the safest, cleanest, and quietest places in America. On the 50th anniversary of his death, his influence can still be seen in local political organizations, publicly-owned Memphis Light Gas & Water, and the sometimes bitter rivalry between Memphis and Nashville.*

Curtain Raiser:
50 Years after Boss Crump

One of the peculiar things about Memphis is its celebrations of the death day rather than the birthday of famous people.

In April, ceremonies mark the assassination of Dr. Martin Luther King at the Lorraine Motel in 1968, and August means "Elvis Week," a gaudy conclave marking the untimely death of Elvis Presley in 1977.

The year 2004 is the 50th anniversary of the death of a Memphian whose influence on the city was as great as anyone's. Just before 5 p.m. on October 16, 1954, a window shade was raised at the home of Edward Hull Crump, signaling to reporters and the crowd on death watch outside that the most powerful man in Memphis and Tennessee politics for half a century had passed away. After turning 80 two weeks earlier, he had died by inches, and obituary writers around the country had plenty of time to polish their work. The Nashville *Tennessean*, which had once called him an "arrogant, vain, vindictive, self-righteous old man" and a "semi-literate old fellow with the steamed-apricot face," gave him a few thousand words. *The New York Times* said "the political scenery becomes a little drabber." *The Washington Post* said "his violent tongue and cynical mind held sway over the lives of the people of an important city."

To his detractors, he was "Boss Crump," a ruthless dictator and enemy of liberalism, freedom and democracy. To thousands of admirers, however, he was "Mr. Crump," the man who turned a corrupt, dirty river town of 100,000 residents at the turn of the century into a prosperous, clean, safe, quiet city of 400,000 people when he died.

The anniversary celebrations are likely to be muted given that most of Crump's political lieutenants and enemies are dead and gone and his influence had been waning since the 1948 elections, pushing him even further back in history. The physical reminders are few. A statue mounted on 80 tons of granite in Overton Park, a road on the southern fringe of downtown leading to the bridge to Arkansas, and a concrete monolith of a football stadium closed 40 years ago and soon to be torn down bear his name. His grave in Elmwood Cemetery draws its share of visitors, as grave sites go. To a generation raised on MTV and to those hard pressed to name the current vice-president of the United States, his name means nothing. But to native Memphians over the age of, say, 60, the mention of "Boss Crump" still provokes vivid memories.

"He was utterly gracious," said attorney Lewis Donelson, recalling a boyhood encounter with Crump on a train in 1932. "I still have a letter that I wrote to my mother saying that I had just met the most charming man I had ever met."

Memphis Flyer politics editor Jackson Baker sold newspaper extras on the street the day Crump died. Crump was "a deity" who strolled the sidelines at football games at Crump Stadium, dispensing candy to the cheerleaders.

From the vantage point of 2004, it seems remarkable that in 1946 Crump's mug — a cartoonist's dream of white hair, bushy eyebrows, twinkling eyes, and round black glasses — was on the cover of *Time* magazine. And he wasn't even mayor, much less a candidate for any high political office, at the time. Only one other Memphian, Holiday Inns founder Kemmons Wilson, has achieved that distinction.

Crump entered Memphis politics in 1902 as a ward leader to the Democratic legislative convention and was elected mayor in 1910. For 50 years he was at various times a councilman, mayor, and congressman. In *Mr. Crump of Memphis*, his biographer, William D. Miller, puts his reign as a true kingmaker and leader of a Memphis political organization with statewide and national clout at about 25 years — from the 1920s until the late 1940s. Memphis mattered in a way it had never mattered before or since.

Crump came to Memphis from Holly Springs, Mississippi, near the heart of novelist William Faulkner's fictional Yoknapatawpha County. He gave Memphis what Faulkner's character Benjy bawls for at the conclusion of *The Sound and the Fury*: order.

"Memphis had a wonderful past, and an iron curtain rang down. Mr. Crump rang it down," said author and longtime Memphis resident Shelby Foote. "Mr. Crump never had a moral approach to government. He wasn't opposed to wickedness or being wicked. But when Prudential Life Insurance announced that Memphis was the murder capital of the United States, that's when Mr. Crump cracked down on the gamblers and the whores and ran 'em out. And Memphis lost a considerable part of its soul when they ran those people out."

Frederick Hoffman, a statistician for the Prudential Insurance Company, stuck the murder rap on Memphis in 1912. For three decades Hoffman sharpened his pencils and compiled annual statistics on the murder rate in U.S. cities — a difficult job then as now because statistics depend on the reporting diligence of various police departments. This was long before the day of FBI crime reports. With 89 murders per 100,000 citizens, Memphis earned Hoffman's "murder capital" rap. The Chamber of Commerce and other local boosters didn't like it one bit. But the numbers made their way from insurance trade journals to the *Literary Digest* to general circulation newspapers where they were hard to ignore.

With the help of a tough police force led by "Holy Joe" Boyle and a notorious public censor of books and movies named Lloyd T. Binford, Crump erased the murder capital label and replaced it with tidy ones like "America's Cleanest City" and "America's Quietest City." Sidney Stewart Jr., who joined the E. H. Crump insurance company in 1950 and served as president from 1965-1981, recalled riding with Crump and his chauffeur when their car came to an intersection as a fire truck approached, horn blaring. Crump instructed the driver to proceed on through because he had instructed all fire trucks to stop for red lights. Wisely, the driver stopped anyway, and the fire truck roared through the intersection before Crump's startled eyes. "Get the number of that truck," he thundered.

The placid Memphis streetscapes were noted by *Time* in its 1946 cover story on Crump: "The city boasted amazingly clean streets, dozens of parks and playgrounds, fine schools, libraries, one of the finest zoos in the U.S., a fairgrounds, an E. H. Crump Stadium, good hospitals, good health."

There was also this paragraph.

"The city was startlingly quiet. Hardly a citizen had tooted his automobile horn in the six years since Crump had banned traffic noise. Lawns were clipped and green; Crump wanted the city to be beautiful. Memphis "niggers" (40 percent of the population) were quiet; and whites, some of whom had negro mistresses, could say contentedly: "No trouble here; no hifalutin' (sic) ideas.""

The fairness of the article and similar ones in other publications is debatable. The quotation marks around the word niggers were in the *Time* story, but it wasn't clear if Crump had used the word or if the author had taken journalistic license. Crump responded to the article by saying, "It seems that the Northern writers are imbued with the idea of belittling the South," a sentiment that would be proven true enough in the years to come. Miller wrote that Crump "never used the word nigger and he did not permit his sons to use it" and shunned racial or religious demagoguery. Blair Hunt, the principal of all-black Booker T. Washington High School who influenced, among others, Memphis Mayor Willie W. Herenton, told Miller that Crump was "a great benefactor to the Negro race." That view, however, has to be tempered by Crump's well-documented distrust of "the intellectual kind" and support of Binford, the guardian of public morals from 1928 until 1955. The board of censors banned Cecil B. DeMille's film *King of Kings* in 1928, the screening of black boxer Joe Louis's fight with Max Schmeling in 1936, the movie *Cabin in the Sky* in 1943 because of its all-black cast, *Imitation of Life* and other movies with interracial themes, as well as *Annie Get Your Gun, Our Gang* comedies, and *Blackboard Jungle.*

Crump and his ally Sen. Kenneth McKellar were key supporters of President Franklin Roosevelt's New Deal and the creation of the Tennessee Valley Authority. Publicly-owned Memphis Light Gas & Water is part of their legacy. Crump's distrust of "the money barons who control the Memphis Power and Light company from their love nests on Wall Street" led to the referendum on November 6, 1934, when Memphians voted 32,735 to 1,868 for TVA and public power — and to mark the occasion named a downtown alley November 6th Street.

But he was neither a liberal nor a populist by a long shot. In 1948 he (and the majority of Memphians) supported the segregationist States Rights candidate for president, Strom Thurmond, over Democrat Harry Truman. Crump's fiercest enemies were liberals such as Edward Meeman, editor of the now defunct *Memphis Press Scimitar*, and Silliman Evans, the owner of the Nashville *Tennessean* in Crump's day. Crump gave as good as he got. Meeman was "Meeman Rat." The *Tennessean's* political favorite, Gov. Gordon Browning, "converted the proud capital of Tennessee into a regular Sodom and Gomorrah, a wicked capital, reeking with sordid, vicious infamy." One of the lasting legacies of the Crump era is the continuing rivalry between Nashville and Memphis, tinged now by race and class as well as the fading memory of Boss Crump.

By the time he died, Crump's brand of order had turned to something he must have viewed with alarm. In 1954, the United States Supreme Court issued its decision on school desegregation in *Brown v. Board of Education.* Elvis Presley, he of the lascivious swivel hips and leers, recorded "That's All Right" at Sun Records. Television spawned a new kind of politician, and, smart as he was, Crump's peculiar Achilles heel was public speaking. Suburban sprawl came with the interstate highway system, and the liberal annexation policies Crump had pushed through the Tennessee General Assembly would never quite catch up to white flight in Memphis. The King assassination in 1968 brought another sticky, unwelcome label to Memphis, "decaying river town," again penned by a writer for *Time.* The murder rate inched back up to a record 213 in 1994. Instead of one all-powerful government and a man to see, Memphis and Shelby County politics are today essentially four governments with two mayors and two legislative bodies, each with an uneasy racial makeup of either seven whites and six blacks or six whites and seven blacks. Between 1954 and 2004, the city that was once famous for getting things done would sometimes seem like the city that couldn't get anything done.

The last of the Crump men in Memphis and Shelby County government was voted out in 1990, but the Crump spirit and something of Crump politics lingers. Willie Herenton, mayor of Memphis

since 1992, was a 14-year-old high school student living near Crump
Boulevard in 1954. Herenton, a former Golden Gloves boxer, occasion-
ally makes news for being feisty with the press and describing political
opponents as being "for sale." Crump once likened political opponent
Estes Kefauver to a "pet coon" and Gordon Browning to Judas
Iscariot. Herenton's current hobby horse is gaining greater control
over Crump's baby, Memphis Light Gas & Water. There was a little of
Crump in two of Herenton's mayoral predecessors, Henry Loeb and
Dick Hackett. Both were known for their personal attention to the details
of public service and grounds keeping and recognized the political
upward mobility of doing a lowly government job well in order to get
a better one.

Mobilizing the Memphis black vote *ala* Crump propelled Harold
Ford Sr., his son Congressman Harold Ford Jr., and a host of Tennessee
Democrats to jobs in Nashville and Washington. It was the lopsided
margins in black precincts in Shelby County — we're talking tallies of
990-2 — that put Tennessee in the Clinton/Gore column in the 1996
presidential election. But they couldn't save Al Gore in 2000. Crump
might have smiled at that. Gore's father, Albert Gore Sr., defeated
Crump's old ally Kenneth McKellar in the 1952 U.S. Senate race.

Finally, there is a note of yearning for Crump, in spirit if not in
name, in the letters to the editor that fill *The Commercial Appeal*
every week, lamenting the current sorry state of things and recalling
the good old days when Memphis was clean, safe, and quiet and had
the awards to prove it. RIP, Mr. Crump.

Sometimes novelists get closer to the essential truth of larger-than-
life characters such as Crump than reporters and biographers can.

There is a scene in Memphis novelist Peter Taylor's story *The
Old Forest*, set in Memphis in the 1930s, where the police chief, newspaper editor, and a prominent man in Memphis society get together
to discuss the sudden and potentially scandalous disappearance of a
young woman in the "old forest" of Overton Park. None of this, of
course, gets in the paper or the police blotter. To Memphians who know
Overton Park, cops, editors, and rich people, that sounds about right.

I have often wondered if Crump was, in part, the model for the
political dictator Willie Stark in Robert Penn Warren's novel, *All the
King's Men*, published in 1946. In his introduction to the Modern

Library edition, Warren rejects the theory that Willie Stark, "the boss," is Huey Long, the real-life Populist governor of Louisiana in the Thirties. Warren said nothing about Crump. But fans of that novel will recall that the narrator, Jack Burden, makes a visit to Lily Mae Littlepaugh's "foul, fox-smelling room in Memphis" to uncover an important clue about her late brother Mortimer which leads to the novel's climax. As a former Nashvillian and Vanderbilt University student, Warren would certainly have been familiar with Crump's career.

In one of the most memorable lines in American fiction, Willie Stark, lying on his death bed after being shot, tells Jack Burden, "It might have all been different Jack, you got to believe that." At the end of the novel, Jack Burden comes to believe that, with all his faults, Stark was a great man. "And believing that Willie Stark was a great man I could think better of all other people and of myself."

Near the end of his own life, Crump, according to Miller, jotted down this note: "I am no accidental character in the game of politics, if I were I would be quickly disposed of . . . God might have made a better berry than the strawberry, but doubtless he never did. There might be a better place to live than Memphis but no such place."

More Power than a
Good Man Ought to Want

(Memphis, 1995; The Memphis Flyer, 2001)

Hickman Ewing, Jr.

A federal prosecutor in Memphis once said that a United States attorney has "more power than a good man ought to want or a bad man ought to have." Hickman Ewing Jr. wielded that power from the late Seventies to the early Nineties. Prosecuting high-profile people like politician Harold Ford, businessman William Tanner, and basketball coach Dana Kirk is a dicey business, and no group of federal prosecutors did more of it than Ewing and his associates. Ewing himself was a controversial public figure considered a conservative zealot by some of his critics. Operating out of Little Rock under Independent Counsel Kenneth Starr, he later played a large part in the Whitewater investigation of Bill and Hillary Clinton, interviewing both in the White House. You can find him in the pages and footnotes of all the Whitewater books, most of which are now as forgotten as Webster Hubbell. In My Life, *Bill Clinton describes Ewing as "just as obsessed as Starr with going after us and not nearly as good at disguising it." Ewing is partially retired and living in Germantown. The federal beat has never been the same. The scarcity and grindingly slow pace of cases involving public officials may be a recognition of the awesome powers of the prosecutor.*

More Power than a
Good Man Ought to Want

Watergate has thrown a thunderous combination. In the 1976 election, Democrat Jimmy Carter, a Georgia peanut farmer, has seized the presidency from Gerald Ford, the Man Who Pardoned Nixon. In Nashville, another son of the soil, Democrat Ray Blanton, is enjoying his second year as governor of Tennessee.

How sweet it is for Blanton, who lost a 1972 Senate race to Howard Baker by 276,000 votes, then came back two years later and whipped Baker's fair-haired protegee, Lamar Alexander, by 120,000 votes. Blanton has a great line about it. As a former congressman, he's proud to go back to Washington to visit his friends. When Alexander, once an aide in the Nixon White House, wants to visit *his* friends, "he has to go to the Allenwood, Pennsylvania, federal prison." It's a real kneeslapper.

In East Tennessee, a handsome young plowboy's-son-turned-banker named Jake Butcher has his eye on the governor's race in 1978 (it was a great decade for Democrats with dirt under their fingernails). Already he is busily exchanging political IOUs with, among others, President Carter and Memphis congressman Harold Ford, who has overwhelmed a Republican opponent and solidified his own growing reputation as a political power broker.

One of President Carter's early official acts is to review the Justice Department's staff of United States attorneys around the country. And the first one he replaces is none other than U.S. Attorney Thomas J.

Turley, a curmudgeonly Republican in Memphis. His successor is a young Democratic idealist and political activist named Mike Cody. Shortly before Cody replaces Turley, the older man takes him aside and offers him a piece of advice.

"Cody, let me tell you one thing," Turley growled. "The United States attorney has more power than a good man ought to want or a bad man ought to have."

More power indeed. Since 1977, that power has shaken Memphis and Tennessee to its good-old-boy foundations. The list of those toppled from their powerful perches by federal prosecutors in Memphis includes Governor Blanton and several cronies; Jake Butcher and his brother, C.H. Butcher Jr.; University of Memphis basketball coach Dana Kirk; Memphis businessman and sports booster William B. Tanner; labor leaders Tommy Powell and the Rev. James Smith; the corrupt institution known as charity bingo; state Representative Emmitt Ford and state Senator Ed Gillock; several of the most crooked and sadistic sheriffs in West Tennessee; and some of the most powerful people in Shelby County government.

The feds also hobbled, perhaps unjustly, former congressman Harold Ford Sr., who might otherwise have become mayor of Memphis. And their investigations fed the demons that drove Shelby County Sheriff Jack Owens and Tennessee Secretary of State Gentry Crowell to commit suicide while at the peak of their powers. Three very different men held the job of United States attorney for West Tennessee over a 20-year period — Tom Turley, a maverick Republican; Mike Cody, a scholarly liberal Democrat; and W. Hickman Ewing Jr., a born-again Christian who later turned his prosecutorial skills against Bill and Hillary Clinton. They turned over a lot of rocks. And what they found gave Memphians a different view of elected officials, celebrities, big-time college sports, and their willingness to empower people who were flamboyant, arrogant, and broke the rules.

By 1976, many Memphis lawyers had frankly had a bellyful of Tom Turley, a self-educated lawyer who chomped on tobacco-loaded dirigibles and kept a portrait of Geronimo behind his desk. "That's the way it's going to be, and if you don't like it," he would say to dissenters, "you can take it up with my assistant." Then he would point to old Geronimo. In the opinion of some equally tough Memphis lawyers of the old school, like Hal Gerber, the son of Boss Crump's famous state prosecutor, Will Gerber, Turley was "difficult." He was the sort of prosecutor who "saw an Indian behind every bush."

Rather than simply take the bank robberies and stolen car cases brought to him by the statistics-mindful FBI and other investigative agencies, Turley and his five-man staff (now there are more than 30 assistants) used the federal prosecutor's special weapon, the investigative grand jury, to poke around. Turley tried to prosecute prominent city and county officials for fraud on a land deal but U.S. District Judge Bailey Brown dismissed the charges. He was known to be looking closely at Harold Ford and at zoning cases involving Democratic Party power William Farris. In the most notorious case of the Turley era, anti-vice crusader Larry Parrish, a Turley assistant, put the stars and distributors of porno-flicks *Deep Throat* and *The Devil in Miss Jones* on trial in Memphis.

Among those with a vested interest in the transition from Turley to Cody were two assistants Turley had hired, Ewing and Dan Clancy. After five years, they were already senior staff. Both expected that they were on the way out. It was common practice for a new U.S. attorney to clean house and install either certified Democrats or certified Republicans, as the case may be. Cody was an unknown quantity as a prosecutor, but his political reputation was well established. At Rhodes College in the 1950s, he had entitled his senior thesis, "An Ethical Politician?" He was a John F. Kennedy fan and a New Frontier idealist during law school, a Carter ally since 1969, head of the Shelby County Democratic Party, Harold Ford's campaign co-chairman in 1974, Carter's Tennessee campaign manager in 1976, and a member of the Memphis City Council.

Now that he was prosecutor, the question was, in Cody's words, whether he would be "the right kind of Democrat." That is to say, one who would soft pedal investigations of prominent Democrats and wink at practices long tolerated. A man who would catch the drift of a timely remark or a phone call or simply the prevailing political winds and act accordingly. He had to prove to Turley's group of protegees that he was not, in the words of one of them, "some politically minded professor of law." The answer was not long in coming. Not only did Cody retain Ewing and Clancy, he made them his top assistants. And the pursuit of public corruption and high-profile cases would be, for the next 16 years, the trademark of federal prosecutors in Memphis.

Turley passed along to Cody and Ewing a favorite maxim about impartiality: Three strikes and you're out, four balls and you walk, no matter who you are. But for all the avuncular wisdom of that Turleyism, a federal prosecutor, then as now, was more like the third prosecutor in an old baseball joke:

First umpire: "I call 'em as I see 'em."

Second umpire: "I call 'em as they *is*."

Third umpire: "They ain't *nothin'* until I call 'em."

During the post-Watergate era, shady practices of long standing became the focus of federal investigations. The public and juries held politicians and government employees to a higher standard. A prosecutor could get an indictment from a grand jury almost at will. Cody's biggest worry was making sure someone wasn't wrongly indicted because "you can't unring that bell."

Watergate gave prosecutors a hunting license. The weapons in their arsenal were the Hobbs Act prohibiting extortion under color of law, the Travel Act, and the Racketeer Influenced and Corrupt Organizations (RICO) statutes. The RICO laws were passed by Congress in 1970 to deal with mob infiltration of legitimate businesses. Aggressive prosecutors used them in public corruption cases after courts ruled that governmental units could be "enterprises" within the meaning of RICO.

Ray Blanton was the most famous Democrat investigated during the Cody years, but for Cody personally, the most fateful case was probably the Emmitt Ford case. Emmitt Ford, a state representative and older brother of Harold Ford, was involved in a scheme to defraud insurance companies. Ewing did the grand jury investigation and Clancy actually tried the case. Cody recused himself but probably wrote his political obituary anyway.

"They (the Fords) held it against Mike," said Ewing. "Mike is a straight-up, totally honest guy. In earlier times, had he not done what was right he might have been mayor."

When Cody ran for mayor of Memphis in 1982, he figured he needed 12 percent of the black vote. He was counting on Harold Ford, whom he had helped elect to Congress in 1974, to help deliver it. Instead, Cody got next to nothing and finished third and out of the runoff between J. O. Patterson Jr. and Dick Hackett. His defeat foretold the future of Memphis politics. The coalition of black and white Democrats that both Cody and Harold Ford had sought to attract was crumbling. An uneasy pact had been broken. Each group was distrustful of the other. For the next 12 years, voting along racial lines would be the rule in Memphis mayoral elections.

Shortly after Ronald Reagan was elected in 1980, Cody resigned. Ewing, as first assistant, succeeded him but didn't expect to be there more than a few months. Rumors began spreading about who the new U.S. attorney would be, and Turley, who still had some clout, asked Ewing if he was interested. He suggested Ewing write a letter to U.S. Senator Howard Baker and say that he had never been a big Republican but was comfortable with the Republican label. Ewing said he would do no such thing. He would submit a resume and that was it. He had gotten along not by knuckling to politicians but by defying them and prosecuting them if they broke the law. Ultimately, Reagan submitted three names. Ewing got the job in Memphis, and his old roommate at Vanderbilt, John Gill, was named U.S. attorney for the eastern district in Knoxville. Two of their old Sigma Chi fraternity brothers from Vanderbilt, Lamar Alexander and Robin Beard, were governor and congressman, respectively. Knoxville was Jake Butcher's stomping ground. The battle lines for the next decade were drawn.

Mike Cody had come to the federal prosecutor's office as a political idealist. His views were tempered by more than a decade of *realpolitik* with politicians and their operatives at every level of government. Hickman Ewing Jr. came out of a different world. He was a Navy veteran and one of the new breed of career prosecutors. He also counted himself part of the 1970s fundamentalist religious renaissance, the born-again Christian. And in a unique way, he had experienced his own brush with Memphis politics.

He grew up in Whitehaven in a family of six children. He was a star athlete and student at Whitehaven High School before enrolling at Vanderbilt but was from the wrong side of the tracks and didn't hang out with the rich kids from East High School and Memphis University School. Maturity hands all sons a different view of their father. The boyhood hero is gradually revealed as the less than perfect man. For Hickman Ewing Jr., the reckoning came in 1964 with the force of an uppercut to the jaw. Hickman Ewing Sr. had been an exceptionally successful high school and college baseball, basketball and football coach and a Southeastern Conference football official. Sportswriters called him "a mentor" of the old school, a builder of character, a maker of men. One of his admirers was Boss Crump, a great football fan. Shortly before he died in 1954, Crump offered two of his favorite coaches, Ewing and Ruffner Murray of Central High School, government jobs.

"You didn't say no to Mr. Crump," said Gerber.

But Murray did. Ewing, however, agreed to fill an unexpired term as county clerk and began a fateful 10-year career in politics. (The clerk's job would later be held by another son of Whitehaven, Dick Hackett.) He was reelected twice, but there were whispers of personal problems and office scandal. Twice Ewing was convicted of drunk driving; a third DUI charge was dismissed. Then in 1964 the roof caved in. Ewing and his office bookkeeper were indicted on charges of embezzling $53,000 over a six-year period. He was suspended as clerk pending trial, then pled guilty several months later to taking $43,000.

"Guilty Plea Gets Ewing 3 Years," announced the *Press-Scimitar* in a headline one inch high. The accompanying photograph showed Ewing being led away by his pastor and a deputy, and the caption read, "On Way To County Jail."

As part of the plea, the popular coach, mentor and father of six was "rendered infamous." In the narrow legal meaning of the term, an infamous person cannot vote or hold office. By far the harsher sentence, as any convicted felon or family member knows, is rendered in the court of public opinion. Ewing was off in the Navy when his father was indicted. He was embarrassed and stunned. When he would come home on leave, he would visit his father in prison but for nearly 15 years he wouldn't talk about it. Father and son finally reconciled and Ewing Sr. even made a successful return to coaching. In 1990 they were together for his induction into the Tennessee Sports Hall of Fame.

"Life goes on," Ewing said years later. "There is forgiveness and there is healing. In Dad's case we always respected him although he had his problems. We had to work through some things but it came out fine. I don't think even subconsciously it's me having the zeal to prosecute public officials because my dad was prosecuted."

Others are not so sure. Whatever the origin of his sense of justice, Ewing was considered an exceptionally driven prosecutor. "I think he had a pretty bad feeling about people charged with violating the public trust," said Gerber. To Arthur Kahn, a former assistant U.S. attorney who worked with Ewing, he was a born leader, immune to political pressure, completely inner-driven. "It's Hick Ewing and his God," Kahn said. "Despite his Christian background, he's not someone with a lot of charity in his heart. His limitation and his genius was his singlemindedness."

Ewing's fundamentalism was both his personal source of strength and frame of reference. He felt like "David going up against Goliath" when he faced the famous Nashville defense attorney James Neal for the first time. He prayed that Neal's counsel "would be turned into foolishness just as the counsel of Ahithophel to Absalom had been turned into foolishness" in the Bible story of King David. His 1980 article for the Law Review, "Combating Official Corruption By All Available Means," began with a passage from the first Book of Samuel:

And his sons walked not in his ways, but turned aside after lucre, and took bribes, and perverted judgment.

Neal, the former Watergate prosecutor, tried several federal criminal cases in Memphis.

"I always found Hick to be honest, extremely hardworking, and ultimately dedicated to his cause," he said. "Some have said he is a zealot, but I think that is too strong. He is a man who sees things as black and white, the very attitude I had during my years as a prosecutor. Hick had never, and has never to my knowledge, spent much time defending the accused and, therefore, would not have had the opportunity to develop the tolerance one acquires when one spends a considerable amount of time, as I now have, defending as well as prosecuting."

Very little is black and white in the politics of a going democracy except the conviction that it is better to win than lose and that, as far as money is concerned, more is preferable to less. Beyond that, the actual business of winning and losing elections, dealing with interest groups, and acquiring money invariably is colored in shades of gray.

By 1990, a major Memphis politician could muster $300,000 or more in contributions before an election and, as Dick Hackett showed, hang on to $348,000 after losing a close election. After Hackett lost to Willie Herenton, white business leaders, by way of atonement, promptly undertook a fund-raising effort on behalf of the new mayor.

Campaign money figured heavily in the political trial of the century in Memphis: the trial of Harold Ford. But there was nothing clearly illegal about the Butcher brothers' financial relationship with Ford that a jury could discern. The case proved to be the West Tennessee division of the Justice Department's Vietnam — a long, costly battle that dragged on for years even after government prosecutors privately believed they would lose. The 10-year investigation ended in Ford's acquittal by a racially mixed jury from the Jackson area. As far as prosecutor Clancy was concerned, the case was lost when it was moved out of Knoxville to Memphis. Read into that what you will. A federal magistrate moved the trial in 1987. In 1990, a jury of eight black and four white Memphians voted 8-4 to acquit Ford on at least one count before U.S. District Judge Odell Horton said juror misconduct made "a mockery" of justice and declared a mistrial. In 1993, with the same lawyers, same key witnesses, and same facts, a sequestered jury of 11 whites and one black from the Jackson area voted 12-0 to acquit the congressman. Had the trial been held in Knoxville, it is Clancy's belief that the vote would have been 12-0 to convict Ford. By this arithmetic, six years and 380 miles of Tennessee real estate equals a 12-vote swing from innocent to guilty.

It was a testament to Ewing's independence that the men respon-sible for removing him from office were a Democrat, Harold Ford, and a Republican, Don Sundquist. Ford, who was under indictment at the time, had minced no words when he ran into Ewing in an elevator in the federal building in 1989 and told him "you are a pitiful excuse for a U.S. attorney but I can guarantee you that you won't be the U.S. attorney much longer."

He was right. On Sundquist's recommendation, Ed Bryant replaced Ewing in 1991 and was in turn replaced by Veronica Coleman in 1993.

"Memphis and Shelby County are pretty clean," said Hal Gerber. "Whether those prosecutions in the Cody and Ewing years had anything to do with it I don't know, but it must have some effect. People must know there is somebody there not afraid to get after their ass if they do something wrong."

After a short stint in private practice, Ewing was once again on the trail of the rich and powerful, this time as a member of Whitewater prosecutor Kenneth Starr's staff investigating President Bill Clinton and Hillary Clinton. From Watergate to Whitewater in 20 years. The names were different — Jim Guy Tucker, Webster Hubbell, Vince Foster, the Clintons — but the themes were familiar: a governor under indictment, corruption, insider deals, a mysterious suicide, a president under siege, cries of partisan politics.

For six years, Ewing ran the Arkansas phase of the investigation that convicted Hubbell, Tucker, and Jim and Susan McDougal. He developed a dead-on impression of Bill Clinton and played him three times in moot court in preparation for the Monica Lewinsky questions which elicited the president's famous line, "It depends on the what the meaning of is is." He was there the day prosecutors brought in Lewinsky's infamous blue dress for the first time. He also interviewed the Clintons several times at the White House. His relationship with his father was the subject of a front-page story in *The Wall Street Journal*, and he was called "Clinton's Other Pursuer" in a long article in *The New Yorker*. The record also shows that he was one of five speakers to eulogize Jim McDougal, whom he convicted.

"I've always said that when you're investigating someone who holds political office, if you don't have the law, you argue the facts. If you don't have the facts, you argue the law. And if you don't have the law or the facts, you attack the prosecutor," he told *The Memphis Flyer* in 2001. "I told Ken Starr, the people that are attacking us, that gives you a clue that maybe they don't have the law or the facts. I told Ken I had been through this many times."

The Trial and Liberation of Harold Ford

(The Memphis Flyer, 1993)

Harold Ford

Harold Ford was tried twice in federal court in Memphis and was under investigation by the federal government for a decade while he was the most powerful politician in Memphis and perhaps in all of Tennessee. I did not know him nearly as well as some older reporters did, nor did I get much of a taste of the famous Ford temper. He was all smiles when he visited the Flyer as part of a victory tour after the second trial, and I have never seen a more charismatic, engaging politician.

My colleague Jackson Baker (and coauthor of this story) and I covered the trial for the Flyer while stringing for national newspapers. There was considerable national interest in the trial and several attempts to pull strings from the Justice Department in Washington. The Wall Street Journal's famous "Who is Webster Hubbell?" editorial was spawned in large part by the run-up to the Ford trial.

Ford is now a political consultant living in Fisher Island, Florida. His son, U.S. Rep. Harold Ford Jr., has his father's charm and quick mind and a more even disposition. Federal prosecutor Dan Clancy is a defense attorney living in Jackson, Tennessee. Judge Jerome Turner died in 2000 from cancer at the age of 57.

The Trial and Liberation
of Harold Ford

I t was not going to be Harold Ford's day. The tipoff came a few
minutes after 10 a.m., in the icy tone, resolute demeanor, and
blunt questions of U.S. District Judge Jerome Turner.

Ellen Meltzer, a lawyer from the Justice Department in
Washington, was gamely explaining how the government would press
the case against Ford with a new jury and without its two prosecutors,
Dan Clancy and Gary Humble, who had just resigned.

"This case is only six years old," Turner said, with an ironic edge
that would have cut steel. And he demanded: "*When* are we going to
dispose of it?"

For reporters in the courtroom, attuned to Turner's nuances, his
tone was a clear shot across the bow. They began calculating the
expanded time or space they would need if the judge should do the
wholly unexpected and deny a motion entered into, in effect, by both
the defense and what was left by the prosecution.

In the dramatic 15 minutes that followed, Judge Turner blasted
U.S. Representative Ford, some of his supporters, the Justice
Department, and at least by implication the White House. By lunch
time, the joint motion had been swept aside and Clancy and Humble,
whose resignations as it turned out had been conditional, were back
on the job.

Ford and codefendants Karl Schledwitz and Doug Beaty were
visibly stunned. The congressman would later that day check into

St. Joseph Hospital with chest pains. Beaty managed some gallows humor. "Make that bourbon!" he said, when a member of the defense team volunteered to go in search of refreshment.

The trial was postponed two days, but Ford's condition could delay it beyond that. At a minimum, jurors — who are not supposed to know any of the latest news about the trial — will have been selected but not sworn in for at least three weeks and in some cases as much as five weeks since they were interviewed.

"I've never seen anything like it in my life," said Jerry Cunningham, the United States Attorney in East Tennessee, where the charges were originally brought against Ford.

Participants' moods underwent a seismic shift during the hour or so that it took Turner to hear and rule on the joint motion. So had the local version of conventional wisdom. At the onset, there had been one main question. Simply put, it was whether a Justice Department newly constituted by the Clinton administration would even bother to pursue trying Rep. Ford with the Memphis-based jury which the motion sought. After all, a 1990 attempt to try Ford with a Memphis jury ended in mistrial, with its eight black and four white jurors at loggerheads and, in the mind of presiding federal district judge Odell Horton, clearly subject to community pressures.

Horton ordered the retrial conducted with jurors selected from a jury pool in the eastern division of Tennessee's Western District, centered on Jackson. When the U.S. 6th Circuit Court of Appeals upheld that decision last year, the way was cleared for jury selection in Jackson. The process was completed two weeks ago with Judge Turner having replaced Judge Horton who had to undergo minor surgery.

During the rancorous jury-selection process, Ford supporters charged in daily demonstrations outside the federal building in Jackson that racism was at work. After both the defense and prosecution exercised their peremptory challenges of prospective jurors, a jury composed of 11 whites and one black was selected.

That racial imbalance was evidently at the heart of a bombshell announcement by acting U.S. Attorney General Stuart Gerson last Friday that the Justice Department would support a defense motion to discharge the jury and start the process over with a jury pool from the Memphis area with its majority-black population.

Gerson acceded to a course that, by all reports, was strongly urged upon him by Webster Hubbell of Little Rock. Hubbell is President Clinton's liaison with the Justice Department, a former law partner of Hillary Clinton, and a man characterized by one political insider as "the guy who's actually running the Justice Department" pending Senate confirmation of Janet Reno, the new president's attorney general designate.

Hubbell had several meetings with Gerson, beginning on February 16th, presenting arguments urged both by Ford and by members of the Congressional Black Caucus. Whether Gerson was actually persuaded by Hubbell or merely went along with what he thought were the wishes of the new administration, he eventually supported the defense argument and ordered prosecutors to follow suit. U.S. Attorney Ed Bryant resigned outright rather than do so. Prosecutors Clancy and Humble withdrew from the case, pending Judge Turner's ruling.

It fell to the unfortunate Meltzer to make the formal case before Judge Turner Monday. The early mood in the courtroom was tense but jaunty. Perhaps Meltzer, like others in the courtroom, expected a pro form ruling by Turner upholding the joint motion, which was made by Ford's attorney, William McDaniels.

If so, she — along with everyone else — was in for a jolt. Turner interrupted her presentation early and often, grilling her about Hubbell's authority, the whys and wherefores of his appointment, and his tenure.

Finally she was reduced to saying, "I think that, I just don't know, your honor."

Turner then turned his attention to the jury selection process and the protests of Ford's supporters.

"Ministers have threatened, without much subtlety, to bring our American system of justice to a halt unless the defendant, Ford, prevails in his effort to seat a jury from Memphis," said Turner.

He blasted "belligerent attacks on the prosecutors, the FBI, and the first judge who tried this case" and the "extreme bias" of Ford supporters at the first trial, reflected in mass gatherings, picketing, traffic slow-downs, and veiled threats from people bused to Jackson.

He noted that during eight days of jury selection, the defense had used its 20 peremptory challenges to strike white jurors and the prosecution struck eight blacks and one white. But he concluded that the challenges were "racially neutral" and that, in the end, the racial makeup of the jury didn't matter.

"A white man is not entitled to a white jury, or to a given number of white jurors. Likewise, a black man is not entitled to a given number of black jurors. A Roman Catholic is not entitled to a jury of Catholics. A Jew is not entitled to a jury of Jews."

He then turned to the Justice Department.

"It is a sad day, in my opinion, when an acting attorney general of the United States and a representative of the White House give into a demand that a jury of the United States must be selected by race . . . that equality depends on one's race."

By this point in the hearing, there was no question where Turner was headed. Schledwitz and Beaty apprehensively caught each other's eye. Ford stared ahead intently but showed no sign yet that his blood pressure was rising and his pulse was racing. But Turner wasn't through with his tongue-lashing.

He said he had never heard of the Justice Department striking a jury. He called political interference with the trial "repugnant to this court's sense of justice."

Finally, he concluded, "I do not believe that there are any facts offered to support this motion or that there is any law to justify its acceptance. It is untimely. It is denied."

Turner ordered a 15-minute recess, during which Meltzer called Gerson in Washington. She would confide later that her superior spoke of the telephone lines "literally boiling over" in Washington. According to one source, Gerson told Meltzer she was "on your own" as to whether to move to dismiss the case without prejudice.

Then Meltzer came back into court. She said Gerson would "take no further action" and indicated that Clancy and Humble, sitting at the prosecution table, would resume their direction of the case. She then asked to be relieved of duty, which she was.

There followed another recess. Ford failed to appear for some time as Clancy and Humble began bringing in exhibits and charts. When Ford finally materialized, Turner called both legal teams to the bench. They returned to their seats for a moment. Ford winced, and McDaniels asked to approach the bench again. Turner talked to McDaniels and Ford, with the others standing by. Spectators could see Ford grimacing and overhear the words "he's sick."

After yet another recess, court resumed with the news from Ford's defense team that he would be hospitalized at St. Joseph's Hospital with evidence of abnormal blood pressure and pulse rate.

It was then that Cunningham, the U.S. Attorney from East Tennessee, and the only prosecutor whose status had gone unaffected through all the trial's tosses and turns, made his statement: "I've never seen anything like it."

Nor had anyone else. But what it all shook down to was this. Although Ford had indeed suffered chest pains, after being tested by a doctor he was pronounced fit for trial. The trial of Harold Ford and codefendants would proceed as scheduled.

In both the local and national press, much was made of Turner's comment that political influence over the Justice Department is "repugnant." The rhetoric surrounding the Ford trial was characterized, on all sides, by generous doses of partisanship and exaggeration. The judge, prosecutors, defense, and Ford supporters were equally guilty on this score.

Throughout Monday's dramatic events, Bryant was one floor below the courtroom, dictating his letter of resignation. He would later acknowledge that he was slated for replacement sometime this year anyway, for partisan political reasons, but insisted his resignation was a matter of principle.

"I probably could have lasted another year," he said. "I was shooting for summertime."

He had decided to resign Friday night after being told by Gerson that the Justice Department was going to side with the defense on the new jury motion.

"This office has always treated defendants equally," he said. "I saw this as an example of an exception being made, and I did not want to be a part of it."

The former unsuccessful congressional candidate said he plans to go home to Jackson and practice law and "get out of the limelight." He wouldn't say if he will get into politics, even though the mention of his name drew a standing ovation at the Shelby County

Republican Party's Lincoln Dinner last weekend. (Note: Bryant did run for Congress and was elected.)

Judge Turner was himself a product of the political process, with all its rough-and-tumble and mutual back-scratching. He was recommended by Republican Congressman Don Sundquist, for whom he served as campaign treasurer. He was formerly a lawyer for Sundquist's business, Graphic Sales. He was appointed to the federal bench by President Ronald Reagan in 1987 and started work in 1988.

The Ford case proved to be the Justice Department's Vietnam. When federal prosecutors and FBI agents across Tennessee began investigating loans to the congressman after the collapse of some 30-odd banks controlled by brothers Jake and C. H. Butcher Jr., in 1983, few imagined it would take four years to get an indictment and more than 10 years for the case to reach a conclusion.

The second trial took six weeks. At times it had an almost nostalgic air. Some of the loans from Butcher banks to Ford were made in 1976. The celebrated "Butcher Bank Collapse," a huge story in 1983, was as distant a memory as the 1982 Knoxville World's Fair and Lamar Alexander's checkered flannel shirt. References to the Butchers as "the Rockefellers of the South" seemed quaint in light of the much larger national savings and loans scandal which unfolded a few years later.

One of the government's star witnesses was Butcher crony Jesse Barr, a self-described expert on bank fraud, whose testimony and roguish personality provided comic relief. Under cross-examination by McDaniels, Barr recounted his fall from grace as a high-paid banker to a government witness with nothing but a dog, his clothes, and his girlfriend.

"My dog died, I've lost so much weight my clothes don't fit, and I ain't too sure about my girlfriend," he said.

In retrospect, the 12 jurors who believed so stoutly in the innocence of Ford would lay heavy emphasis on the absence of C. H. Butcher Jr., from the proceedings.

"Government, why did you not call Mr. C. H. Butcher? Where are you, Mr. Butcher? Outside the door?" mocked defense attorney Herbert Moncier in his closing argument.

In a bold move that contrasted with his first trial, Ford himself decided to take the stand, uttering a memorable deadpan "Good Morning, Mr. Clancy," to the prosecutor who had stalked him for so many years.

A damning revelation, a fit of nerves, or a burst of the famous Ford temper could be fatal to his case. In preparation for the moment, Ford's attorneys subjected him to weeks of simulated cross-examination. To discipline himself, Ford wore the same dark grey suit for 71 days, rose each morning at 5:30, and remained virtually expressionless in the presence of the jury. "Take the blows," Ford's attorneys advised him. It was conceded that Clancy would score some points about the Ford funeral home, loans from the Butcher banks, and Ford's personal financial irresponsibility. But when they came, Ford deadpanned his way through simple "that is correct" answers.

The upside was that Ford got to paint a sympathetic picture of himself as a hard-working young man in a family business and as a congressman who was not afraid to face federal prosecutors. The positive image was magnified when prosecutors declined to call the Butchers and were unable to effectively tie Ford to the Auction Street bridge to Mud Island, which the Butchers had once hoped to develop.

"You heard Butcher this, Butcher that, Butcher Butcher Butcher all through the trial. If he was so important he should have been there," said juror Timothy Grace from Decaturville.

For their part, looking back on the case, Clancy and Humble would suggest that the key moment occurred long ago when the trial was moved from Knoxville to Memphis. Ford raised more than $1 million for his defense through local fundraisers and the efforts of the Congressional Black Caucus. Some 50 supporters along with his son, Harold Ford Jr., helped pack the courtroom each day and several hundred rallied for a petition drive designed to take the hopes of Memphis for a National Football League team down to perdition with him should he be found guilty.

During almost seven weeks of being sequestered in Memphis, the jurors from assorted rural corners of West Tennessee saw little of the big city. Mainly they would walk the corridors of the Ramada Inn or gather to play checkers. They were forbidden, of course, to talk to each other about the trial prior to starting their deliberations.

Juror Danny Montgomery, a hog farmer from Ramer, was

surprised when he later learned about Ford's concerns about getting a fair trial from a mostly-white jury.

"He should have given us a chance to judge him before he judged us first," he said. "But I can see his point, too. Evidently, there is a lot more racial tension in Memphis than where we live. But I think Mr. Ford and the people of Memphis have found out that white people from the country can be fair."

The Last White Mayor

(Memphis, 1995)

Dick Hackett

Dick Hackett and I were born one week apart in the month of July in 1949, he in Memphis, me in Western Michigan. We each grew up in close families, had good throwing arms, and dreamed of being baseball players. I occasionally run into him downtown, where he is director of the Wonders Series, and we talk about our college-age children and politics in that order. We are friendlier now than we were as daily newspaper reporter and mayor for eight years, when I found him one of the toughest interviews in town. Because he was young, came from Whitehaven, and did not graduate from college, Hackett tended to be underestimated. He was funny, smart, and a quick study to begin with, and his confidence, speaking ability, and political skills increased on the job. I often wonder what would have happened to him and to Memphis if he had been elected mayor when he was 43 instead of when he was 33.

The Last White Mayor

T he most amazing thing to happen in Memphis politics in the
last 25 years was Dick Hackett losing the mayor's race. Second
most amazing was Dick Hackett winning the mayor's office.

When he lost to Willie Herenton by 142 votes in 1991, Hackett
was 42 years old, had nine years of on-the-job experience, $600,000
of campaign funds, a fistful of endorsements, and got 49.4 percent of
the vote. When he slipped into a mayoral runoff in the special election
of 1982, Hackett was 33 years old, had been county clerk for four years,
had less than $100,000 in campaign funds, hardly any endorsements,
and got 30 percent of the vote.

Both his defeat and victory required a combination of extraordinary
events. Hackett probably would have won in 1991 . . . if only 72 people
had changed their vote from Herenton to Hackett . . . if only 2,923
people had not voted for crackpot candidate Robert "Prince Mongo"
Hodges from "Planet Zambodia" . . . if only Hackett had spent some
of that $348,000 in leftover campaign funds . . . if only a federal judge
hadn't just abolished mayoral runoff elections in Memphis.

He never would have won in 1982 . . . if only Mayor Wyeth
Chandler had not resigned . . . if only three lawyers had not forced the
city to hold a special election . . . if only there had not been a majority-
vote requirement in Memphis mayoral elections.

How to account for such an unusually star-crossed political
career?

"In Memphis, you need to know two things," Hackett said five years after his defeat. "You need to know your numbers and your colors."

Numbers and colors. Black voters and white voters who took the trouble to register and go to the polls. In the end, that was all that really counted.

But if a mayoral election was little more than a glorified census count, with political volunteers instead of census workers doing the counting, what was a mayor for? What of the years between elections? And what made a good mayor or a bad one?

In short, the problem with the numbers-and-colors explanation is that it sells Hackett short as a flesh-and-blood politician, administrator, and leader capable of both wisdom and mistakes. And it was never smart to underestimate Dick Hackett, who never lost an election until 1991. Everyone who ran against him or thought about it claimed to have more of something — experience, education, vision, fresh ideas, cross-racial appeal, charisma. There was Mike Cody, Mr. Democrat, and City Council eminence J.O. Patterson Jr. in 1982; black candidates John Ford and D'Army Bailey in 1983; Bill Gibbons, Mr. Young Republican, and Minerva Johnican, a female black independent in 1987; and Jack Owens, Mr. Drug Fighter, before his suicide in 1990. None could beat Hackett, and most wound up supporting him in future races.

For nearly two decades as a mayoral assistant, county clerk, and mayor, Hackett resonated with the majority of Memphis voters by being thrifty, dependable, hard-working, and bland. His remarkably efficient career had its beginnings in a solid, orderly Whitehaven household once described by one of the ex-mayor's brothers as "Ward and June's" after the parents in the 1950s television comedy *Leave It To Beaver*. Hackett came by his keen eye and his thriftiness early. When his father gave him five shotgun shells to go hunting, he was expected to come back with five rabbits. He graduated from Hillcrest High School in Whitehaven, leaving scarcely a trace of his presence in the high school annuals of the mid-Sixties. City schools were being gradually desegregated; busing and massive white flight were yet to come.

He attended Memphis State University for the better part of three years, but his government know-how came from experience, not out of a textbook. He got a job in Chandler's successful 1971 mayoral campaign. Chandler was the first Memphis mayor elected after the annexation of Whitehaven by the city, and he wanted some Whitehaven representation in his administration. Chandler picked Hackett to run the city Information and Complaint Center, later called the Mayor's Action Center. It was probably the most formative experience of his political life. "It helped me relate to the everyday problems of services or lack of services from city government," he would say later.

Government could do big things like run a school system and a police force, but it also did a lot of little things like garbage pickup and permits and license plates. As a young citizen advocate, Hackett found he enjoyed a surprising amount of publicity. At the time, television stations and two daily newspapers were running consumer assistance columns and programs called "Action Line" or "Action Please." Hackett was literally "Mr. Action," with his own radio show and a growing collection of favorable press clippings. The problems of public education, crime, and race relations were messy and often seemed insurmountable. The Action Center was a government oasis where positive results could be seen — and counted — right away. After a few years, Hackett was ready for bigger things. When Chandler wouldn't make him director of the division of sanitation because he was too young, Hackett "walked straight over to the Election Commission and filed for clerk" in 1978.

He won, and immediately set about trimming the office staff by 20 percent and cutting the budget by 30 percent. That put him at odds with the public employees union, but there was no political downside for a conservative white politician taking on a mostly black union. "Wouldn't it be great if all of our elected officials had so much consideration for our tax revenues?" gushed a newspaper editorial under the in-your-fantasy headline, "More Hackett Types Needed."

In 1982, Chandler made a deal with then-Governor Lamar Alexander that he would resign and Alexander would appoint him to a judgeship. The vacancy would be filled by an appointed mayor who would fill the remainder of Chandler's term and keep a grip on the office for the next four or five years. But a 30-year-old lawyer named Dan Norwood had other ideas, and filed a lawsuit demanding an election "on behalf of the citizens of Memphis." After a hectic eleventh-hour court battle, Norwood prevailed.

Dick Hackett as clerk was one thing, but Dick Hackett as mayor was something else. *The Commercial Appeal*, the city's surviving daily, and the business community shunned him in favor of the more worldly Cody, a lawyer, former federal prosecutor, and former City Council member. But Hackett managed to turn that to his advantage, too. "I played up big-time Mike Cody being the fat-cat candidate," he said. "I did not believe the polls. I never thought there was grassroots support out there for Mike." Hackett and his campaigners made sure voters knew that Cody was divorced, a supporter of the American Civil Liberties Union and the NAACP, and former political ally of Harold Ford.

Patterson led the field with 41 percent of the vote to 30 percent for Hackett and 26 percent for Cody. In the runoff, Hackett got 54 percent of the vote, roughly the percentage of white registered voters in the electorate.

In the 1983 mayoral election, he got 132,460 votes, a record to date. From the middle of 1982 to the end of 1983, he won no less than three city or county elections — one for clerk, and two for mayor — and finished second but in the money in a fourth. That is a record unmatched in local political history.

And he did it as an independent. There was no local party primary until 1992, sparing Hackett from having to identify himself with either the Republican Party, as Don Sundquist and Jim Rout did in their formative years, or the Democrats as Mike Cody did. No other city or county politician, with the exception of former Shelby County Mayor Bill Morris, so successfully navigated the middle ground.

After 1983, a funny thing happened. The notorious homebody became a regular globetrotter, albeit with a package of crackers and peanut butter in his suitcase lest the native vittles prove too exotic. In tandem with Morris, and joking that they saw each other once a day at 4 a.m. when Hackett was getting up and Morris was going to bed, he courted International Paper and set up a recurring world-class cultural exhibition, the Wonders Series. He reluctantly signed on to The Pyramid and the expansion of Liberty Bowl Memorial Stadium, knowing they would cost him politically. The Memphis Zoo and downtown mall were overhauled, St. Jude Children's Research Hospital locked in to a future in Memphis, and the old Midtown expressway corridor was redeveloped.

Still, Hackett was thrifty, maybe too much so. To keep from raising property taxes he did everything but sweep the change off the city's dresser, dipping into various reserve funds. He pushed but one property tax increase, leaving his successor, Herenton, and the City Council little choice but to pass two more in 1992 and 1994. And the inability of Hackett's political strategist, Shelby County Assessor Bill Boyd, to complete a property reappraisal from 1982 to 1988 meant that homeowners were, in effect, paying taxes on pre-inflation 1970s real estate values.

Hackett was also fortunate to be mayor during the quietest decade in Memphis since Boss Crump. There were no crises on the order of the public employee strikes or school desegregation protests during the Chandler administration or the Martin Luther King Jr. assassination during the Henry Loeb years. But the 1980s in Memphis were not, by a long shot, the 1950s. Thousands of "Ward and June" households left places like Whitehaven for places outside the city limits. There was a quiet crisis, a troubling sense that things were slipping away, and a gradual loss of confidence in the city's future. County government took on more and more public functions as consolidation proposals flopped and annexations were bottled up in court or by official inaction. From 1980 to 1990, Memphis lost 5.5 percent of its population. The metropolitan area, true enough, grew by 7 percent, but metropolitan Nashville grew by 16 percent, Charlotte by 20 percent, Atlanta by 32 percent, and Orlando by 52 percent during the same time.

The one number future historians are likely to remember about Dick Hackett is 142. Hackett insists he put more time into the 1991 election than any other and refuses to second-guess himself for leaving those campaign funds unspent and later at his personal disposal. He said he could have spent 15 cents and it would not have made any difference. Had he been reelected, he said he would have run for governor in 1994 as a Republican. Instead, he went to work for St. Jude and later for the Wonders Series. Like thousands of his former constituents, he and his family left Whitehaven for a home in East Memphis and later moved to DeSoto County, Mississippi.

"I loved my work, took it as a ministry, but it was not a political thing for me," Hackett said, claiming a purity of motives that is pure Hackett. One regret he confessed to was not being invited to Herenton's 1992 swearing-in ceremony, although the oversight was corrected four years later and the two became quite cordial. Memphis was denied the inexpensive satisfaction of a symbolic handshake at the first inauguration and would have to work out its salvation, if possible, by more strenuous means.

Willie Herenton and his Critics

(The Memphis Flyer, 2004)

Willie Herenton

By 142 votes, Willie Herenton won the closest, most exciting mayoral election in Tennessee history in 1991. He can lay claim to the title of Memphis' Longest Running Newsmaker, with 12 years as city school superintendent and 12 more and counting as mayor. After all those years in the public spotlight, there is a side of Herenton nobody knows, which partly accounts for his uncanny ability to anger citizens and members of the City Council at a time when he ought to be basking in accolades. Like other reporters, I have seen that side up close. I once referred to the mayor as stubborn in a story, and he strenuously objected that the term was condescending and racist. A few years later I heard him use it to describe himself, but I guess that's different.

Willie Herenton and his Critics

Make no mistake. The name of the game now is "Get the Mayor." As in, get him out of office. Things are that bad between the mayor and the City Council and a growing legion of Herenton opponents.

City councilman Jack Sammons and his pals at *The Commercial Appeal* have called for a "Watergate-style investigation" of the mayor's role in the selection of lawyers and underwriters for a $1.5 billion TVA bond deal with Memphis Light Gas & Water. They have likened the mayor to Richard Nixon and Bill Clinton. And they probably thought twice about Saddam Hussein.

Just a few months ago, it seemed that Willie Herenton could be mayor of Memphis for as long as he wanted to be. The city's first elected black mayor. The city's first mayor to serve four consecutive terms. Mayor for life — and now mayor for the moment. What happened? Some historical perspective helps explain.

First, Mayor Herenton is neither as popular nor as unpopular as is widely believed. In 1991, he upset incumbent Dick Hackett by 142 votes in an election in which 247,973 people voted, or 65 percent of the electorate. Last October, Herenton beat John Willingham three-to-one, but only 104,688 people voted, a 23.7 percent turnout.

That's a lot of apathy. The signs began popping up four years earlier. In the 1999 election, Herenton's opponents on the ballot got 54 percent to his 46 percent. But there were so many of them that

Herenton won easily. Under pre-1991 rules, he would have been in a runoff.

The 1991 election amounted to a crusade, with Jesse Jackson and then-Congressman Harold Ford Sr. playing key roles and other black politicians, ministers, and voters almost unanimously behind Herenton. "There was an emancipation fervor among the people," Herenton has said. Shortly after taking office, Herenton was visited by his pastor, the Rev. James Netters, one of the first black members of the Memphis City Council. Netters said he had a vision of Herenton as a healer, "the only person who can heal Memphis."

In the first month of his fourth term, a majority-black City Council rejected four Herenton nominees for director jobs. And Herenton was determined to replace the leadership and board of MLGW.

But Herenton is not as unpopular as this controversy suggests. Politics is always an either-or choice. There is no evidence that Sammons, Rickey Peete, Tom Marshall, or Carol Chumney could beat Herenton one-on-one. Sammons, Willingham, and Joe Ford are among the elected officials who have learned the hard way that their appeal is limited. Only Harold Ford Jr. or A C Wharton have the stature to challenge Herenton.

The weekly drumbeat of anti-Herenton letters to the editor and talk-show comments reflects a suburban demographic. When these missives go beyond the standard "Memphis is going to hell under Herenton" message, the "facts" cited are often wrong. A Memphis police officer from Bartlett, for example, wrote about "increasing crime." In fact, between 1996 and 2003, rapes declined 27 percent, robberies 29 percent, business robberies 9 percent, aggravated assaults 15 percent, and homicides 24 percent. Our source? The Memphis Police Department and District Attorney General Bill Gibbons.

In 1996, *Memphis* magazine gathered mayors Herenton, Hackett, and Wyeth Chandler together for a photograph and three long stories. Chandler advised Herenton to be a strong mayor, to conciliate individual council members but keep the council as a body at bay. "You're the one who's got to be the cook," he said. "Not those other folks in the kitchen."

Hackett followed that advice and stuck mainly to goals that were achievable. Herenton's proposals, on the other hand, made great headlines but nearly impossible policy: consolidate city and county governments, abolish the school board, sell MLGW, rebalance city and county taxes. And far from conciliating individual council members, Herenton has antagonized and insulted them.

In his book about leadership, *Certain Trumpets*, writer Garry Wills said that what great leaders have in common is followers and the ability to move them toward a goal. Wills contrasts each of the leaders he profiles with an anti-type, an often famous person who seems to embody some of the qualities of leadership but ultimately lacked followers. In his first two terms, Herenton led Memphis through what could have been a turbulent period of transition from white mayor to black mayor. In his fourth term, he risks becoming one of Wills' anti-types.

"They call me King Willie on the radio," he said with a laugh. "If I were King Willie, we would not have a lot of the problems that we have because I would rule decisively. But I'm just one elected official. I can't wave a magic wand. If I had the authority and the power, the school systems would be consolidated, the governments would be consolidated, and we would have casino gaming."

He cannot lead within the limits of his powers when he said in another interview a few months later, "I'm not looking for friendship on the council. I'm looking for a cooperative working relationship to move this city forward — and respect. I don't need no damn friends on the council."

The present focus on Herenton's supposedly Nixonian exercise of political influence in the bond deal is absurdly myopic, partisan, and narrow. The $25,000 steered to a Little Rock law firm wouldn't pay the food and bar bill at a major East Memphis Republican political pony-up, and everyone on the council knows it. But no one said politics is fair.

Chuck Daly, one of several former head coaches who have worked for the Memphis Grizzlies, once said something very wise about leaving the Detroit Pistons after winning two NBA championships. "Sooner or later, they just stop listening to you."

After 12 years, that's what's happened to Mayor Herenton.

II.
Gamblers

Charles McVean,
the Hackney-Pony Man

(The Commercial Appeal, 1989)

If something is repeated often enough in the newspapers, people will start to believe it, all evidence to the contrary. Such is the case with gambling in Memphis, which is often said to be unconstitutional, politically impossible, or both. In 1987, the General Assembly passed a bill allowing parimutuel betting by local option. Memphis voters approved horseracing by a 3-2 margin a few months later. In 1989, Charles McVean came within two votes on the Tennessee Racing Commission of being Tennessee's first gambling impresario. McVean planned to race miniature hackney ponies mounted with robot jockeys in indoor arenas. Charity bingo and horseracing proposals were serious business in Tennessee in the 1980s only a few years before casinos came to Mississippi.

In 1990 McVean came very close to going to prison when a jury split 6-6 on bribery charges stemming from the General Assembly's approval of horseracing. A mistrial was declared. Over the objections of some federal prosecutors, McVean was not retried in either state or federal court. He went back to trading commodities, and his firm, McVean Trading, is one of the most successful in the South.

Charles McVean,
the Hackney-Pony Man

I t's 20 miles and a world of difference from the sleek Ridgeway office complex in East Memphis to Speedy's place on Crump Boulevard, next to an inner-city housing project.

Ridgeway houses the office of Charles 'Chas' McVean, the hackney pony man. Two small brick buildings at 271-277 Crump house Speedy Drive-In Liquors and Speedy's Amusements. Speedy is J. P. 'Speedy' Murrell, owner of the buildings.

They are also headquarters of two McVean-Murrell partnerships called Concerned Citizens for Better Government and Inner City Development Agency. It's "a good marriage," said Arnett Montague, president of the two groups.

Some marriages match people seemingly as unlike as can be. This is one of them.

McVean is a wealthy, white, Vanderbilt-educated commodities trader who sponsors a philosophy symposium at his college alma mater. Murrell is a black small-businessman and ex-convict with little formal education, lots of street savvy, and a reputation as a political power broker.

What brought these two together? The answer sheds some light on Memphis politics and provides a glimpse into why efforts to win legalization of hackney pony racing are being investigated by a grand jury and why the ponies won't be racing in Memphis any time soon. And in a way it has to do with the "Stealth Taurus" and Mr. Ed, the talking horse of television fame.

To hear McVean tell it, the hackney pony — once bred to pull carriages or "hacks" — is the most exciting racing equine since Secretariat. Mounted by remote-controlled robot jockeys, McVean's hackneys speed around small indoor tracks in less time and with greater frequency than thoroughbreds, hence increasing the number of wagering opportunities. McVean likens the power and excitement of the hackney pony to Herschel Walker bursting through tacklers on the way to the end zone. Others who have seen the exhibition races or videos call it one of the more ridiculous spectacles in the vast panoply of American trash sports.

The Stealth Taurus is what McVean calls his car, which appears to be an ordinary Ford Taurus, a sculptured sedan likened by some to a rolling jelly bean. Inside, however, is an array of computerized electronic gadgetry and under the hood is a monster customized engine. The Stealth Taurus can go from zero to 60 miles an hour in less time than it takes McVean to anger a Tennessee racing commissioner, which is to say about four seconds.

The surprises in the Stealth Taurus are sort of like the surprises in McVean himself, a pleasant, bespectacled man known to his old friends from Vanderbilt and East High School in Memphis as 'Chas.' Brash and plainspoken, McVean warms to people who remind him of himself. Jerry Williams was an old boyhood friend who liked to boast of the politicians he knew in Memphis and Nashville. McVean hadn't seen him in years until they met outside a Memphis hotel following a stormy session between McVean and thoroughbred racing backers prior to the 1987 referendum on racetrack betting.

McVean and the thoroughbred crowd disagreed on a lot. One thing was the advertising campaign featuring Mr. Ed, a relic of the Sixties when television generally pretended that black people did not exist. Black support was crucial to McVean's plans, and he thought TV and newspaper advertising, speeches to civic clubs, and a campaign based on Mr. Ed failed to reach many of them.

Williams told McVean he could help. He claimed to have been working for a company called Information Network Systems but was actually padding his resume. The company did not exist. But Williams knew a little about horses and he knew arenas and booking agents from his days working for the Sixties rock group Paul Revere

and the Raiders. And he knew a political wheeler-dealer named
J. P. Murrell.

McVean agreed to pay Williams $10,000 a month plus expenses
to be his consultant. Williams made the introduction to Murrell, who
had worked for both the mayor of Memphis, Dick Hackett, and the
mayor of Nashville, Richard Fulton. For years, white politicians have
hired black consultants to help spread their name in the black community through endorsements, sample ballots, bumper stickers, and
poll workers on election day. U.S. Rep. Harold Ford and his brother,
state Sen. John Ford, are the best known. With money to burn and a
do-or-die referendum that would determine the fate of horse racing in
Tennessee, McVean paid $90,000 to Murrell and Montague, $70,000
to John Ford, and made a $15,000 contribution to Harold Ford's legal
defense fund.

Murrell got his business start and his nickname years ago when
he worked for Speedy Radio and Television Repair at 271 Crump. In
the Sixties, he entered the amusements business and took over Gaia's
liquor store next door. He did well, and in the Seventies he bought a
house in the South Parkway East neighborhood where such prominent
black Memphians as Maxine and Vasco Smith, Michael Hooks, and
A C Wharton live. In 1979 he was indicted in Nashville in the
clemency-for-cash investigation of former Gov. Ray Blanton. The
charges were dropped after a witness, Tennessee Alcoholic Beverage
Commission agent and photographer Ernest Withers refused to testify.
But he was convicted later that year on a federal charge of extorting
payoffs from a nightclub owner selling illegal liquor. The license for
his store is held by his wife.

The referendum was a smashing success for McVean. With overwhelming support in black precincts, Memphis voters approved
parimutuel wagering by a 3-2 margin. McVean and his new friends
celebrated at The Peabody, where he told anyone who would listen,
"This is a mandate!"

When the battle shifted to the Tennessee Racing Commission,
McVean kept Murrell and Montague on the payroll for $15,000 a
month as his "community relations agency," rejecting the advice of
establishment consultants that he limit his contributions to groups
with more financial accountability. Inner-City Development talked

about rebuilding an old movie theater on Lamar and other community projects such as distributing food baskets to the needy. But, to McVean's surprise, its focus was really on Fayette County which borders Memphis and Shelby County on the east and has a black population of just over 12,000 compared to 310,000 for Memphis. Fayette County's leading citizen is influential state Senator and Lt. Governor John Wilder, who got an $8,000 contribution from McVean via Murrell and Montague. Montague teaches at Fayette-Ware High School and said he adopted the school as a charity. He and Murrell and friends arrived at graduation ceremonies in a limousine.

Herman Cox, the president of the Fayette County NAACP, accused school officials of using students as a front to advance gambling.

"The citizens of this county knew nothing about the alleged monies that were supposedly being spent for low-income citizens," he said. "It is highly inconceivable that such a large amount of money is being spent for school activities without the knowledge of Fayette County citizens."

The referendum and a front-page story in *The Wall Street Journal* that followed proved to be the highlight of McVean's horse racing career. McVean's impulsive spending caught up with him. In January, a lobbyist named W. D. 'Donnie' Walker pleaded guilty to charges of trying to bribe a state senator to vote for the horse racing bill in 1987. A key piece of evidence was McVean's $24,000 check to Walker dated April 28, 1987 — the day before the state Senate voted for legalization by a single vote.

"The price was high, but my back was against the wall," McVean said.

From 1983 to 1987, Walker was the state's chief regulator of "charity" bingo, a form of gambling that is legal if it is conducted by charitable organizations as a fund-raising tool. Tennessee has had as many as 200 bingo operators licensed by the Secretary of State's office. Walker pleaded guilty to state bribery charges and federal charges of extortion and tax evasion stemming from payoffs from bingo operators.

In spite of all that, McVean still had a chance, maybe even a good chance, had he not antagonized the most influential member of the Tennessee Racing Commission, Nashville attorney James Neal. They snapped at each other at a public hearing at the Mid-South Coliseum, and in private made no effort to hide their disdain for one another. McVean could hardly have picked a tougher adversary. Neal played college football at the University of Wyoming and looked like the jut-jawed Marlboro man. As a young federal prosecutor in the 1960s, he helped Attorney General Robert Kennedy and the U.S. Justice Department convict labor leader Jimmy Hoffa. Years later, Neal delighted in telling stories about how Hoffa gave him the finger every day in court and tried to get him to "come outside and let's you and me settle this thing in the gym." Neal was not a man to be intimidated. Nor was he opposed to letting Memphis work out its own destiny. He was a good friend and admirer of fellow lawyer and racing commissioner Lucius Burch. During the public hearing, Neal slipped a note to a reporter for *The Commercial Appeal.*

"What does your employer think?" it read.

"Give it a shot," the reporter wrote back, and Neal silently nodded.

A few weeks later the commission voted 5-2 to deny McVean a license. One of the ayes came from Burch. A two-vote swing and McVean would have had his license. Simulcasting and slot machines could well have come next. Had that happened, the hackney pony might well have been put out to pasture in favor of thoroughbreds and McVean himself bought out by one of the big public companies that own the thoroughbred tracks on the East Coast and West Coast. But to do that, he would have had to have kept his mouth shut and his money and checkbook in his pocket.

And neither of those things were possible when Chas McVean was under the spell of hackney-pony madness.

Half Pregnant with the Tennessee Lottery

(*The Memphis Flyer*, 2002)

Senator Steve Cohen

Lawmakers can overcome nearly any impediment if they put their minds to it. From 1834 until 2003 when it was amended, Article XI, Section 5 of the Tennessee Constitution said, "The Legislature shall have no power to authorize lotteries for any purpose, and shall pass laws to prohibit the sale of lottery tickets in the state."

Thanks in large part to the legislative efforts of Sen. Steve Cohen of Memphis over nearly two decades, Tennesseans began playing their own state lottery in 2004. As in neighboring states Kentucky and Georgia, a share of the proceeds is funding college scholarships for 50,000 students. By mid-year, ticket sales were falling steadily each month but still totaled $355 million. While the restrictions on casino gambling in Tennessee appear to be ironclad, at least two efforts are underway to bring an Indian-owned casino to Memphis and Shelby County, which is struggling to finance bonded indebtedness of $1.4 billion.

Half Pregnant
with the Tennessee Lottery

Tennessee took considerable pains to become half-pregnant. This is what happened when the lottery amendment passed on November 5th and the General Assembly subsequently approved a state lottery for college scholarships. The state is officially in the business of promoting, marketing, and profiting from gambling. At the same time, it must more adamantly than ever oppose the form of gambling that has had a much greater impact on Tennesseans, especially Memphians — casinos.

The main reason the proposed lottery amendment took up so much space on the ballot, right below the governor's race in the left-hand column, was to erect legal blockades in front of anyone with ideas about a lottery being a gateway to casinos, particularly Native American casinos like the ones run by the Choctaws in Neshoba County, Mississippi.

Gamblers being forward-looking sorts, there was a little buzz during Tunica's 10th-anniversary celebration about the chances of a tribal casino in Memphis if the lottery amendment passes.

The reasoning went something like this: Casinos quietly entered Mississippi through the back door while the governor and everyone else were diverted by a lottery issue that never went anywhere. Once established, riverboat or dockside gambling soon evolved into something high and dry and many times larger than anyone envisioned.

Memphis is looking for a major tenant for The Pyramid now

that the Grizzlies and the U of M Tigers are leaving for the FedEx Forum. Pyramid debt service looks more and more like a $3 million-a-year albatross. The Pinch District, always an underperformer, will be more forlorn than ever. The Pyramid's neighbor, Mud Island River Park, is also underused and would be an interesting site for a casino.

Memphis and Shelby County residents spend $300 million to $400 million a year in Tunica, compared to the estimated $243 million that all Tennesseans together spend on lottery tickets in Georgia and Kentucky. If lotteries in neighboring states are a leak, casinos are a flood.

Deed Mud Island or The Pyramid to the Chickasaw Indians and set them up under provisions of the Federal Indian Gaming Regulatory Act, just like their brethren the Choctaws in Mississippi or the Pequot in Connecticut. Suddenly, casinos are 30 minutes closer to Memphis.

What's wrong with that scenario?

"No way" it can happen, said lottery proponent Sen. Steve Cohen. "No Indians and no Tigers, Bears, or Orioles, either."

But the question is hardly off the wall. The Tennessee attorney general's office addressed the state lottery and the Indian Gaming Regulatory Act (IGRA) in two opinions in early 2001.

"Because Senate Joint Resolution 01 expressly states that it does not authorize games of chance associated with casinos, it would not be a gateway to Indian casino gambling in Tennessee," the opinion read. "The state would not be required to negotiate with an Indian tribe about casino gambling, nor could the tribe sue the state without its consent to force the negotiation."

End of story? Probably but perhaps not. One of the interesting things about the proposed constitutional amendment is how it breaks down one gambling barrier while erecting another.

Quoting from the attorney general's opinion, "Currently, the Tennessee Constitution, Article XI, section 5, flatly prohibits the General Assembly from authorizing lotteries. The constitutional provision does not, however, prohibit all types of gambling. Except for lotteries, there is nothing in the state constitution prohibiting gambling, and the regulation of all types of gambling, other than lotteries, is a matter for determination by the General Assembly."

As the opinion notes, Tennessee law already provides for parimutuel betting. In fact, in 1987, Memphians approved a horse-racing referendum for a parimutuel track that was never built. The legal rule of thumb is that bona fide tribes can engage, on their sovereign lands, in whatever forms of gambling are allowed in the rest of a state. But in addition to the ban on casinos in the amendment, there are strong doubts whether the IGRA applies to Tennessee.

"To this office's knowledge, there is no Indian tribe which holds Indian land in Tennessee," the attorney general's opinion read. "Thus, at this point, IGRA does not apply."

In other states, however, tribal claims have suddenly been made when casinos are on the horizon. An incomplete Internet roster of "Native American Associations" in Tennessee has 89 listings, with a caveat that some are probably defunct or fake. For several years, Native Americans have held an annual powwow at Halle Stadium in Memphis.

Lottery proponents, who didn't wish to complicate their long-sought amendment with any more controversy than necessary, took no chances. So the word "casino" was added to the amendment and, voters willing, to the state constitution but in a negative sense. And now that businesses all over the state are selling lottery tickets, the state of Tennessee is in the odd position of promoting instant scratch-for-cash tickets while busting the criminals who operate gas-station pinball machines or video poker.

Mississippi casino interests profess to be bored by the whole thing.

"We don't have an official position," said John Osborne, president of the Mississippi Gaming Association and general manager of Hollywood Casino in Tunica. "Most people believe the residents of Tennessee need to make that determination."

Casinos and a lottery coexist in New Jersey, he noted. One school of thought holds that lotteries take players from casinos, but Osborne views Tunica as a destination resort offering amenities and gambling experiences "you really can't get at a gas station."

How Tunica Became the
New Las Vegas

(Memphis, 1996 and 1997; The Memphis Flyer, 2003)

The bad luck and recklessness that sank Charles McVean and
Memphis in their quest for legalized gambling was Mississippi's good luck.
Casino gambling came to Mississippi through the back door while the governor and legislature were preoccupied with a state lottery bill that never
passed. It revitalized Mississippi's Gulf Coast and made Tunica, once a
byword for poverty, an entertainment center for the Southeastern U.S.

The phrase "Mississippi riverboat gambling" is misleading short-
hand. Only in Natchez does a boat actually sit in the Mississippi River.
The rest are either in the back bays or waters of the Mississippi Sound or
in back channels or man-made lagoons along the Mississippi River. To the
casual eye, they are indistinguishable from land-based casinos.

How Tunica Became the
New Las Vegas

T wo things, we have been told by sainted Alabama football coach Bear Bryant, legions of preachers, and the authors of a hundred country weepers, are sacred in the South: Momma and Sunday morning. So what did thousands of Southerners do this year on Mother's Day, a Sunday?

Took Momma to the casino, that's what.

The mainstream appeal of casinos is transforming the Mississippi Delta and making Memphis handmaiden to an entertainment industry category-killer not of its making. It is happening with breathtaking speed and on a scale even bigger than the eye-popping excesses of professional sports. After a lengthy public debate and referendum, Nashville spent $290 million on a new stadium for the Houston Oilers, now the Tennessee Titans. A single casino project that opened in June, Grand Casino Tunica, will ultimately cost upwards of $450 million, all privately financed. In all, nine Tunica County casinos have spent well over $1 billion in the space of, historically speaking, about 15 minutes. In the 1589-page *Encyclopedia of Southern Culture*, published in Oxford, Mississippi in 1989, there are two entries for clog dancing, five for cockfighting, and eight for cotton gins. There are none for casinos.

The slot machine is changing Mississippi more than any invention since the cotton gin. The irony is that all this is taking place in a part of the world once famous for poverty, cotton, and the slow, almost immeasurable pace of change. Tunica's economy, and to a lesser extent Memphis', was built on cotton. Ben Robertson called cotton "the greatest crop heaven ever gave" in *Red Hills and Cotton*. For generations of Southerners, it provided clothes, money for education and housing, even a platform for political campaiging. In the Mississippi Delta, King Cotton has been overthrown by the Casino Empire. Flat fields where cotton once grew now sport towering neon signs, gaudy casinos, and parking lots full of thousands of cars. Stretch limousines and tour buses are far more common on area roads than farm machinery. Two months before Grand Casino opened, there were so many trucks, bulldozers, and cranes reshaping the landscape that it looked like a military operation.

The most vivid demonstration of how the market was revalued came in 1993 in a law office in the First Tennessee Bank building. Shea Leatherman, a wealthy Tunica cotton farmer, was selling 150 acres to Boyd Gaming Corporation, owner of Sam's Town Casino and Gambling Hall. At the time, Splash Casino was taking in millions every week and the land rush was on. Las Vegas casino owner Jack Binion had bought a big parcel in the north part of the county and brought in Circus Circus and ITT Sheraton as partners. Boyd Gaming was fearful of missing the Tunica action.

Leatherman hoped to get a few million dollars for land that would have fetched less than a million a year or two earlier. Instead Boyd offered $20 million. Leatherman and his agent somehow managed to keep a straight face and settled for $25 million. In its first full year of operation, Boyd Gaming's Sam's Town Tunica had revenues of $128 million and operating income of $33 million.

Casino gambling may or may not be harmless entertainment. It is assuredly bad for compulsive personalities who get hooked on it, as thousands do. It may prove damaging in the long run to feeder markets like Memphis and Helena, Arkansas, that supply customers but don't get any tax revenue. And it may be bad for local markets like Greenville that rely too much on nickel players and nearby residents.

But the evidence is overwhelming that legalized casino gambling has been good for the state of Mississippi, which is enjoying a boom in construction, tax collections, tourism, and conventions at the expense of Tennessee, Arkansas, Florida, Louisiana, and Alabama. Those five states provide over half the customers in Mississippi casinos. Memphis and Shelby County alone contribute an estimated $400 million yearly, which is more than the entire operating budget for the city of Memphis.

There are 29 Mississippi casinos, including $700 million Beau Rivage on the Gulf Coast and the 31-story, 1,200-room Gold Strike hotel and casino in Tunica. They employ 33,000 people, plus thousands of construction workers. By the end of 1997, five years after the first casino opened, the state had collected over $1 billion in gaming taxes. Added to the $3.4 billion the state got from its settlement with the tobacco industry, the revenue will allow Mississippi to provide services it could not otherwise have provided. Ironically, the double sin-tax windfall lets Mississippi have its cake and eat it too. Casinos are one of the last bastions of smokers' rights. Not since the glory days of Ole Miss football coach John Vaught and the heyday of southern Democrats in Washington's seniority system has Mississippi enjoyed such national prominence in anything besides John Grisham novels and the poverty index.

An economic boom, of course, is most obvious in an economically depressed area. And in the 1980s, Mississippi was depressed. All but one of the coast's hotels were in receivership. Tunica was one of the poorest counties in the country, as Jesse Jackson pointed out in a well-publicized visit to the infamous "Sugar Ditch" neighborhood. County supervisors all over the state were being brought up on corruption charges.

And Mississippi's jackpot is partly due to a chain of political events in other states that could hardly have been scripted any better, at least from Mississippi's point of view. Missouri, Iowa, Illinois, and Louisiana stuck a toe in the waters of riverboat gambling, opting for high taxes, restricted hours, betting limits, and limited licenses. Tennessee and Alabama stayed out altogether. Mississippi dived in headfirst.

Luck was on their side, but Mississippi lawmakers, regulators, and casino operators made decisions that were smarter, bolder, and ultimately more profitable than competitors, often against the advice of experts and moralists. Again and again, the skeptics who said the "nation's fiftieth state" was too small, too conservative, too religious, too isolated, or too unregulated were wrong.

A comparison of riverboat gambling in Mississippi and Kansas City in 1997 illustrates Mississippi's advantages. In Kansas City, there is a $500 loss limit per visit. Drinks cost $3 and must be paid for in cash, not chips. There are no ATMs on the floor of casinos. Slot machines are not fitted with bill acceptors. And the boats are permanently anchored but players have to get in line for a two-hour "cruise" and get off and reboard to play some more. Most important, Missouri has a 20 percent tax on the gaming win. Mississippi has a 12 percent tax. Kansas City did $318 million in gambling revenue in 1996, while Tunica County casinos, with roughly half the population in the surrounding area, did $750 million.

The differences are due to two bills that passed the Mississippi Legislature in 1990.

"It never would have happened in the light of sunshine," said Dr. Arthur Cosby, director of the Social Science Research Center at Mississippi State University and founder of its Gaming Research Group.

Mississippi has no constitutional prohibitions on casino gambling. Constitutional amendments require a two-thirds vote of the Legislature and a statewide referendum. Only a simple majority of the Mississippi House and Senate was needed to legalize riverboat gambling. In the 1980s, the focus was on a lottery, which had the support of Gov. Ray Mabus. Several lottery bills were introduced but they failed. In 1989, the legislature permitted cruise ship gambling in international waters of the Gulf of Mexico, but this proved unpopular because of all the restrictions.

In 1990, the House Ways and Means Committee created a special subcommittee on casino gambling. It crafted a bill that allowed casinos in counties along the Mississippi River in addition to the Gulf Coast. Once a casino application was filed, the burden would be on opponents to force a referendum in the county to ban gambling, as they have done twice in DeSoto County adjacent to Memphis.

Lawmakers themselves were not aware of the size of the industry they were creating.

"We were looking for sources of revenue," said Rep. Charlie Williams (R-Senatobia), a member of the subcommittee. "But there was no consensus on an income tax or sales tax. Casinos never had to go to a statewide vote. If that had been the case, it never would have passed. The 'antis' were focused on lotteries. The cat was out of the bag before they started chasing it.

"Our projections were way too low — three boats on the coast, three on the river, and 3,000 total employees, with $18 million to the state. We were so overwhelmed by those figures that we agreed to talk about $10 million because no one would believe $18 million."

Williams favored limiting licenses to get companies bidding against each other. But subcommittee chairman H. L. "Sonny" Merideth insisted on open licensing. Merideth and Bobby Long, an attorney for the State Tax Commission, modeled the bill after the laws of Nevada and New Jersey.

Because it was a gamble for a company to come to Mississippi, license fees were kept low, and taxes set at 12 percent — roughly 8 percent to the state and 4 percent to the counties with casinos. When the bill came to the floor, Williams was asked about Tunica. He mentioned the history of riverboats in the Delta and the proximity of Tunica to Memphis.

"I'm sure," he added confidently, "that they will never have more than one."

The bill passed the House and Senate. Ten of 52 senators "took a walk" or were absent, lowering the total number of votes needed for passage. Still, it passed the Senate by only two votes. Mabus signed the bill and, later that year, a companion bill creating the gaming commission without so much as a signing ceremony.

In retrospect, Merideth said he was pleased with the law and its administration, but asked if he anticipated its impact, he replied, "Good God no, I still don't understand it."

The former lawmaker, now a lawyer in Greenville, can see the power of legalized gambling, for better and for worse, at three casinos in his hometown.

"There's too much money going to gambling that should be going to groceries," he said. "You can walk through the crowds and tell they've got people gambling that should be home cutting the yard. From the state's standpoint, it's clearly been a plus across the board. It remade the coast."

Mabus had generally positive feelings about the impact of casinos.

"The bottom line for me was, I was willing to take a chance. What we had been doing clearly wasn't working as well as it should have. That and the local option were the main reasons I signed the bills."

The former governor said he was under no pressure from either gambling proponents or opponents to sign or veto the bills, but when he put the modest sum of $10 million in projected gaming revenues in his final budget in 1992, "I was just pummeled every which way by the media, the legislature, and everyone else" who thought the sum fanciful. It was right on target.

It was two years from the passage of the bill to the opening of the first three dockside casinos on the Gulf Coast. Their success, along with Splash in Tunica, encouraged bigger operators to come to Mississippi in 1993. The expansion of gambling in Tunica could not have happened, however, without a crucial vote by the three-member Mississippi Tax Commission on August 4, 1993. At that time, four casinos were operating in Tunica County at Mhoon Landing, right next to the Mississippi River and a full hour or more from Memphis. None of them had hotels. A dozen more casino companies were poised to go forward north of there, pending site approval from the commission. The issue was whether casinos could move inland as much as 3,000 feet via canals between the river and man-made ponds that housed the floating "riverboat" casinos. (Even now, there is subtle metal strip of gangplank that marks the entrance to the casino from its adjoining hotel lobby.)

If the answer was yes, then the monopoly of landowners Dick Flowers and Dutch Parker at Mhoon Landing would be broken and the industry would move to Robinsonville and Commerce Landing, 20-30 minutes closer to Memphis.

"It made every bit of difference in the world because it was all tied to Wall Street," said Sam Begley, a Jackson attorney who argued that the new sites should be approved. "It unleashed $500 million in investment immediately after that."

The decisive vote on the commission was cast by Harvey Johnson, a lawyer who later became the first black mayor of Jackson. Paul Battle, the influential president of the Tunica County Board of Supervisors, wanted the commission to approve the new sites. During more than three hours of presentations and debate, Commissioner Ed Buelow warned that "we're fixing to build a Grand Canyon." He voted no. Commissioner William Tann voted yes, leaving it up to Johnson. "From a practical standpoint, we need to move forward, so I would vote in favor of the motion," he said.

Replied Buelow, "Needless to say, I think we move forward. I think we moved into Pandora's box, and we've opened it up for good." Harrah's Entertainment, which had urged the Mississippi Gaming Commission to limit licenses and tried unsuccessfully to get approval for a casino in DeSoto County just across the state line from Memphis, made the first move to Robinsonville. Mike Rose, president and CEO of Harrah's Entertainment in 1993, was a veteran of the expansion of casinos into New Jersey in the Seventies. On a brilliantly clear morning, he stood outside the doors of Harrah's in Robinsonville watching a line of cars that snaked a mile or so over the levee and into the parking lot waiting for the grand opening.

"Unbelievable," he muttered.

For a while, Mississippi was opening a new casino every two weeks. By 1997, 30 of them were operating, grossing over $2 billion in revenue. The full impact of the 1990 legislation was evident in the 1996 national elections. Gambling opponents, rallying around crusading Methodist minister Tom Grey and the National Coalition Against Legalized Gambling (NCALG) defeated casino proposals in 23 out of 25 states, including Arkansas and Florida. The fledgling organization was exultant.

"This year's round of battles over gambling is finished, and the winner is: NCALG!" its newsletter boasted.

Actually, there were two winners. As far as Mississippi was concerned, the NCALG might as well have been the political arm of the state tourism and visitors bureau.

The success of casinos in Mississippi and other "backwater" states fulfilled the vision of Harrah's founder Bill Harrah. Philip Satre, Rose's successor in 1994, worked for him as a lawyer from 1975 until Harrah's death in 1978.

"What Bill Harrah saw after World War II was that the gaming business couldn't grow and sustain itself if it relied only on gamblers," Satre said. "He expanded the concept into showrooms, big-name entertainment, restaurants and hotels. Tahoe and Reno are the only two places he ever operated. He opened the Tahoe hotel in 1959. He as

able to enjoy the Squaw Valley Olympics in 1960 as a way of promoting his business. He also recognized that the industry would have
strong appeal to people with time and money on their hands. So he
developed the programs for older people. At one point Harrah's was
the largest user, next to the armed services, of Greyhound Bus Lines.

"And the third thing he did was recognize that slot machines
could be a powerful driver of the business. We were criticized through
the 1980s as being a slot joint. We believed slots were both the growth
side and the most profitable side of the business, and we reaped
enormous profits."

A slot machine is the most efficient money-making machine that
mathematics and electrical engineering ever devised. You don't have to
feed or water it. It doesn't get retirement benefits. It doesn't drink, take
coffee breaks, go on maternity leave, or go to the bathroom. It does its
own marketing and works 24 hours a day, seven days a week. Tunica
casinos earn, on average, more than 80 percent of their gambling revenue
from slots. A new machine costs $6,000 and pays for itself in about
a month.

There were 11,114 slot machines in Tunica County by 1996, or
1,000 more than the number of residents. They earned $58,819,149
in the month of March. To put that in local perspective, cotton yields
in 1995 in the Mississippi Delta, according to Cotton Council
International, were about 700 pounds per acre. At the benchmark
high price of $1 a pound, cotton earned $700 an acre after being
planted, subsidized, sprayed, irrigated, prayed over and harvested. A
2,000-acre farm might earn $1.4 million a year — or about what 18
slots earned in the same time.

The hold, or the win percentage, is what the casino wins. The
payback is what the players get back. Mississippi law requires the
payback to be at least 85 percent. That means slots pay back, on
average, 85 cents for every dollar put in. While this is true for the uni-
verse of players, it does not hold for individual players, just as flipping
a coin 100 times may not produce 50 heads and 50 tails. The more
competitive the market and the higher the coin value, the "looser" or
more generous the slots. "Loosest slots in Tunica" is largely a matter of
billboard hype and gamblers' mythology. A casino can have a few
$100 machines set to pay back 100 percent or even more some months,

but the other machines are not as loose. One of the most instructive exercises for casino patrons is watching through the plate-glass windows of the casino count room where coins and tokens are weighed for the "hard count." One hundred pounds of $1 tokens is worth $2,180; 100 pounds of $5 tokens is $6,084; and 100 pounds of nickels is worth $455. Then they move it around on steel pallets with industrial fork lifts.

It was not Harrah's that made the biggest or best bet in Tunica. The Memphis-based company, an offshoot of Holiday Inns, never seemed really comfortable there, closing its first location and buying the failed property of another operator less than a mile away. Harrah's would eventually close its Memphis headquarters and move to Nevada.

The master strategist of Tunica gambling was a bald, open-faced newcomer named Jack Binion. In a business full of men with wet, slicked-back hair and cool demeanors, Binion spoofed his "aw shucks" everyman appearance in television commercials and newspaper advertisements that belied his skill as a land developer and political operator. He became Tunica's first celebrity, unable to walk through the casino without attracting customers who wanted to slap him on the back or shake his hand.

Binion saw his family-owned casino in downtown Las Vegas, Binion's Horseshoe, miss the action as the business moved to The Strip and to Laughlin, Nevada.

"I'm not going to miss it this time," he vowed after visiting Splash shortly after it opened.

He bought 242 acres of land near Robinsonville for $1 million from G.A. Robinson III (no relation to the town's namesake). Then Binion brought in ITT Sheraton for $6 million, and Circus Circus for another $6 million, which he split 50-50 with Sheraton. On land deals alone, Binion was up $8 million before the Horseshoe in Tunica opened. And his site was closer to Memphis than Harrah's and Boyd Gaming's Sam's Town. Boyd had offered Binion $8 million for a site next to Horseshoe the day after he made his deal with Sheraton and would later buy its site for $25 million.

"I left $2 million on the table," Binion moaned to Robinson.

"I'm the wrong person to tell that to," said Robinson, who had sold for $1 million.

Binion later gave him an ownership interest in the casino. Binion also bought another 1,225 acres of protected land east of the levee which can be developed as housing, a golf course, a factory outlet mall, or a NASCAR track.

Along with church groups, Horseshoe led the successful opposition to legalized gambling in DeSoto County which would have threatened Tunica. DeSoto County is mostly white and known for its wholesome atmosphere of schools and churches. One of the highlights of the casino campaign was a widely distributed flyer featuring a photograph of the jewelry-draped black owner of a Tunica juke joint named Van Siggers in which he urged DeSoto County voters to approve gambling so that he could open a casino the size of several football fields on the Coldwater River deep inside the county. The referendum resulted in gambling being overwhelmingly rejected.

With less floor space than its Tunica competitors, Horseshoe boasts the highest revenues and profits, according to the Mississippi Gaming Commission and industry reports. A vintage 1950s red Cadillac limousine with a set of longhorns for a hood ornament sits in front of the casino as a tribute to Jack's father, the late Benny Binion, a Texan who set up shop in Las Vegas in 1946. Horseshoe revels in its image as a no-nonsense gambling hall and poker parlor where dealers get the best tips, high-rollers the best odds, and poker players the chance to rub shoulders with pros and get a shot at the World Series of Poker, now televised on ESPN. Publicity about a Binion brother with drug problems and mob ties and a lawsuit in which Jack Binion's sisters claimed his separately owned Tunica and Louisiana casinos steal customers from the family-owned Vegas Horseshoe have not tarnished the image at all.

In 2003, eleven years after the first casino opened in Tunica County, Jack Binion sold Horseshoe Gaming to Harrah's Entertainment for $1.45 billion.

The Schillings Make a Splash

(Memphis, 1996)

Ron and Rick Schilling

The first casino in the northern part of Mississippi was Splash Casino in Tunica, once one of the poorest counties in America. Operators Rick and Ron Schilling had worked in their father's Ohio River nightclub, The Beverly Hills Supper Club, which was destroyed in a fire in 1977 that killed 164 people. Splash was nothing but a low-slung nightclub built on top of barges but it made $40 million for the Schillings and convinced big-time operators to enter the market. Even today, however, Tunica struggles to keep its population above 10,000 although the county's annual take from gambling taxes is roughly $42 million a year.

The Schillings live in Fort Lauderdale. Rick Schilling is part of a group that is applying to operate a new casino in Greenville. The ruins of Splash, less scenic than the ruins of antebellum mansions but no less historic, can still be seen at Mhoon Landing, 15 minutes south of the present casinos.

The Schillings Make a Splash

Mhoon Landing is about as desolate as the face of the moon. Four years ago this ugly piece of Tunica County floodland, pockmarked by man-made lagoons the size of football fields, was thought to be the most valuable property in the state of Mississippi. Then its luck abruptly changed.

This is where the aptly named Splash Casino and two casino novices, Rick and Ron Schilling, now living in the lap of luxury in Fort Lauderdale, provided screaming proof of the raw power of legalized gambling in a virgin market.

Casinos in Mississippi, Las Vegas, and Atlantic City spend hundred of millions of dollars these days on hotels, theme parks, restaurants, and even replicas of New York City. Splash, a refurbished disco on a barge, opened October 19, 1992, without restaurants, entertainment, or a single hotel room. It overcame a comedy of errors including exploding toilets, flooded parking lots, two closings and fines by the Mississippi Gaming Commission, feuding owners, and a local official hell-bent on shutting the whole thing down.

And it literally made so much money they couldn't count it fast enough. In 1993, hundreds of gamblers stood in line for hours to pay $10 for the privilege of losing their money at Splash. Lines of cars a mile long snaked across the levee to get into the parking lot. Slot machines earned an average $480 a day.

Today all of that seems as distant and fantastic as the riverboat tales of Mark Twain or the ghost towns of the Old West. Casinos are thriving in Tunica County, but the action all moved north, closer to Memphis. Mhoon Landing is an environmental wreck, horribly scarred, and as deserted as it was before the casinos came. The boats are all gone. All that's left is the detritus of foregone development — a mostly empty trailer park, a couple of abandoned buildings, and a nearly new $1.7 million road to nowhere.

Gambling is all about winners and losers. Mhoon Landing was Tunica's first big loser. The Schillings, who owned half of Splash, were its first big winners, taking more than $20 million apiece out of Tunica's first jackpot.

Today you can find them among posh Fort Lauderdale's idle and not-so-idle rich. Rick is married, mellowed, and gives little hint of the hard-driving management style that once earned him an unflattering nickname that rhymes with Rick. A non-drinker for several years due to pancreatitis, he resembles the actor John Goodman in girth and appearance. Ron is the classic single guy in paradise — great tan, gold chain, sports car, fancy house on one of Lauderdale's inland waterways. His only Splash memento is a singular piece of three-dimensional wall art of a bare-breasted woman in a seductive pose.

Business partners since they were teenagers, "Ricky" and "Ronnie" as they call each other, moved to Fort Lauderdale for the good life and to be close to their parents, who will celebrate their 50th wedding anniversary this year. "Ricky," his brother explains, "loves to do deals." Offer half or even one-fourth of the asking price and see if they take it. In Lauderdale's fantasyland, you never know. Like the boat Rick just picked up for $600,000. He doesn't even like boats. But his wife does. Already they have a 40-foot speed boat called Linda Sue's Splash.

"This is not a boat, this is a bleeping ship," Rick said of his latest acquisition as he attacks a rack of lamb at an Italian restaurant. The Schillings can clean food from a plate faster than gravity. "The guy wanted $3 million. It's 105 feet long. This thing can make 20,000 gallons of fresh water a day. Can you believe it?"

"Tired and retired," Rick has no plans to reenter the casino business. Not so younger brother "Ronnie." He recently moved Splash's stripped and vandalized barge from Mhoon Landing to Vicksburg to overhaul it and put it back in service. By fall he hopes to be operating a new casino in Natchez, just below the Ramada Inn and the bridge to Louisiana. "I want to go after that Baton Rouge business," he said, eyes sparkling. Having failed to get a casino license in Indiana, he is now exploring casino ventures in Russia and China. The Chinese joint venture has been licensed but, so far, unable to attract an investor. "There's $60,000 merchant marines and 20 million people in the area and we haven't got an investor," Ron sighs.

He said he is — no kidding — the gaming commissioner of China, the most populous country in the world, a happenstance he himself seems to find fairly improbable.

But no more improbable than Splash. Big casino operators like Harrah's and Binion's Horseshoe passed on Mhoon Landing in 1991 and 1992. Memphis and DeSoto County were still possible sites, and there were several miles of river frontage north of Mhoon Landing in Tunica County. "When gambling got in, everybody just sat there," said Jack Binion. "They threw a party and nobody came."

The first time the Schillings and their father saw Mhoon Landing it was underwater. On opening night it rained so hard the tents and awnings blew down. Still hundreds of people stood in line. "I said wow, what a business," recalled Rick.

The Schillings had worked in family-owned restaurants and nightclubs on the Ohio River from the time they were boys. Their father owned the Beverly Hills Supper Club in Southgate, Kentucky, just outside Cincinnati. A fire at the club killed 164 people in 1977. According to the Life Safety Code Handbook of the National Fire Protection Association, the club was overloaded to more than twice its capacity.

The brothers eventually overcame that tragedy and operated several other large and popular riverboat restaurants. The Mississippi Gaming Commission routinely licensed them. But a Tunica County building inspector and retired engineer, Clint Nickles, remained skeptical of "the goddamned Schillings" as he called them and was a thorn in their sides until he died in 1994.

Nickles, a crusty, jug-eared Mississippian dubbed "Mr. Magoo" by engineers who dealt with him, shared his concerns about road signs (he wouldn't allow Splash to put them up in Tunica County), safety, overcrowding, and floods with both regulators and reporters. He was the only person in Tunica County trying to stop the runaway train. The one thing that the Schillings weren't about to have was another fire. One key employee said the sprinkler system at Splash was so powerful that "if there was a fire you would have drowned."

Space, or the lack of it, was a constant concern. With no competition for nearly a year, Splash's slot machines were earning over $300,000 a day. The Schillings crammed as many machines as they legally could on board whenever they sensed any weakness in Nickles' position. Once the restaurant opened, the Schillings were constrained by having it on the boat instead of a landside facility. But food, especially center-cut New York strip steaks, was a Schilling specialty and helped Splash dominate its market even after Bally's, Lady Luck, and The President casinos opened nearby.

Architects drew up plans for several hotels and restaurants. But the partnership, which included the Schillings, the boat builder, the first financier, the landlords, and the daughter and son of the men who dreamed up the whole thing, couldn't agree on them. The minority partners balked at the Schillings' plan to buy a second riverboat called the Spirit of America. Not even crisis could unite them when there was a buck to be made. Landlord Dutch Parker, a wealthy Tunica planter and tractor dealer who made two percent of Splash's gross revenue, once drove up to the casino as workers were stacking sandbags to hold back a spring flood. He offered to provide a pump — if they would rent it for a few hundred dollars a day.

The tent that served as an entertainment center moved three times. The offices, for a time, were in a trailer on the site. Another office building was a metal horse barn that the Schillings acquired from a customer. Once a contractor mistakenly installed a force pump instead of a flush pump to a toilet in a trailer, resulting in a spectacular polluted geyser that showered, among others, Rick Schilling.

Maintaining the supply of currency, coins, and tokens was another problem, especially on weekends. Slot machines literally ran out of tokens. A "drop" — opening and emptying a machine — had to be authorized by the Mississippi Gaming Commission. Confusion over special drops resulted in the second closing and fining of Splash by the Gaming Commission. "No one ever told us we needed so many tokens," said Rick Schilling. "Our business plan was only $50 million a year."

In the count rooms, bills would be bound and stacked like bales of cotton. Every Friday, Splash would get $100,000 in $100 bills because everyone wanted to get paid off in $100s although they played with $20s. A security service rushed the weekend's winnings straight to the Federal Reserve Bank in Memphis. "Sometimes bags would have as much as $3 million to $4 million in them on weekends," said Herb McMillan, Splash's first chief administrative officer.

It lasted about a year. Then two things happened. DeSoto County voters said no to gambling for the second time, effectively assuring that Tunica would be the epicenter of the casino industry in this region. And in a landmark decision, the Gaming Commission decided that a lagoon at the end of a canal a few thousand feet from the Mississippi River met the definition of a navigable waterway. Splash, in contrast, was right next to the river. The big money moved into Casino Center and Casino Strip, still in Tunica County but 15 to 20 minutes closer to Memphis, and Splash's number was up.

An unsung hero of Splash was a mechanical wizard and general Mr. Fix-it named Danny Malone. A hard-working Irishman, Malone would don a pair of coveralls and do whatever had to be done to keep the boat working and, quite literally, afloat. At the bitter end, the Schillings rewarded him by naming him the last chief executive officer of Splash. In the final days, a visitor found Malone royally ensconced in a massive office built for one of his more pretentious predecessors. He was wearing a big grin and a tie that came down about six inches below his neck. There were papers all over the huge mahogany desk, and on top of them a Skil Saw.

By then the Splash partners were barely on speaking terms. The Schillings tried to sell out to a poker machine distributor called International Gaming Management, which was going to do a public stock offering of Splash and two other Mississippi properties. Before that could happen, IGM was busted by the United States Attorney's office for connections to organized crime. Ron Schilling said he had another offer for $500 million but the partners wouldn't take it. The Schillings, in turn, refused to sell their interest to two of the other partners.

Splash closed on May 24, 1995. Mother Nature kept throwing sevens that spring, and finally the parking lot flooded. But by then Bally's and Lady Luck had already pulled out of their lagoons (at a combined cost of over $22 million), and Mhoon Landing was a lost cause. Never ones to shun a little hard work or stiff a customer, the Schillings rolled up their sleeves and helped the kitchen crew with the grub. "They kept the steaks coming to the very end," an ex-employee said grudgingly.

Splash cost $23 million and paid for itself in about 60 days. In its best year, it grossed $170 million, which is more than any of the bigger, fancier properties have done since.

"They say extreme profits always lead to extreme competition," Rick Schilling said with a shrug, tooling around Fort Lauderdale behind the wheel of a new Lincoln. Let the others fight over the Tunica market. Ricky and Ronnie did alright.

III.
King Assassination
Conspiracy Theories

James Earl Ray and the Amazing Tupper Saussy

(The Memphis Flyer, 1998)

Tupper Saussy

On April 4, 1968, the Reverend Dr. Martin Luther King Jr. was assassinated in Memphis while standing on the balcony outside his room at the Lorraine Motel. James Earl Ray pleaded guilty after his capture in 1969, then recanted. In 1978, the House Select Committee on Assassinations concluded that Ray was the shooter but might have had help.

Before he died in prison in 1998, Ray convinced members of the King family and others that he was just a pawn or innocent. He had help in this undertaking from conspiracy theorists with media savvy, writing skills and their own agendas. One of them was Tupper Saussy, who ghost-wrote a book for Ray called The Tennessee Waltz. *Saussy, a former song-writer and advertising executive in Nashville, was a federal fugitive tax protester at the time. He talked for the first time about his involvement with Ray, his past, and his life on the lam in an interview for* The Memphis Flyer *a few weeks after Ray died.*

James Earl Ray and
the Amazing Tupper Saussy

Perhaps the greatest King-assassination conspiracy theorist of
them all was mysteriously missing in the blizzard of coverage
last month of the death of James Earl Ray.

There is a fitting irony to that because Frederick Tupper Saussy
III was mysteriously missing, period, for 10 years after ghostwriting
Ray's book, *The Tennessee Waltz*, in 1987. The 61-year-old former
songwriter and Nashville socialite was convicted of failing to file
income-tax returns in 1985. Two years later he disappeared days before
he was supposed to begin serving his prison term. Last November he
was apprehended in Venice Beach, California.

Saussy is partly responsible for the belief among King-assassination
conspiracy theorists, including members of the King family, that Ray
was an innocent patsy. The notion that Ray, an eighth-grade dropout,
wrote a book as literate and philosophical as *The Tennessee Waltz* is
preposterous to anyone who ever interviewed him, heard him interviewed on television, or read excerpts of his unedited letters to author
William Bradford Huie that were the basis for the book *He Slew the
Dreamer*. Yet this canard was solemnly repeated in all of Ray's obituaries,
as well as by people who should have known better, like conspiracy
debunker and author Gerald Posner.

In an eight-page letter and an interview with the *Flyer*— the first
he has given since going on the lam — Saussy admitted his role in the
strange transformation of Ray from assassin to political prisoner. After

pleading guilty in 1969 to King's murder at the Lorraine Motel, Ray
soon recanted and unsuccessfully sought a trial. For the next 29 years
until his death last month, he put forth various conspiracy theories
and persuaded, among others, King's family, the Rev. James Lawson,
and several Memphis ministers of his innocence.

In the mid-1980s while imprisoned in Tennessee, Ray apparently
became aware of Saussy's anti-government views from newspaper stories
about his trial. He sent Saussy a typed postcard asking if he would help
write his autobiography.

"Both Ray and King were sacrificial victims," Saussy said. "I never
asked James why he chose me, but I believe he sensed a common
denominator among the three of us."

There followed a box of 175 handwritten pages that became the
basis for *The Tennessee Waltz* — a book stylishly edited and generously
interwoven with Saussy's own literary, intellectual, and philosophical
musings. Saussy denied authorship in a foreword to the book, but
now admits he wrote parts of it himself and rewrote or edited the rest
based on interviews and letters from Ray.

"I deliberated prayerfully over whether I should claim credit for
'as told to' status, and concluded that James had been taken advantage
of by enough vain mercenaries," he said.

As it turned out, Ray did not return the favor. After the book was
published by Saussy in 1987, Ray disavowed parts of it and sued
Saussy. The lawsuit was later dropped, but a makeover edition of *The
Tennessee Waltz*, retitled *Who Killed Martin Luther King?*, was later
published. It too ran into controversy because of unauthorized blurbs
on the cover. Newspaper columnist Carl Rowan, King associate Andrew
Young, and King's son Martin Luther King III told *The Washington
Post* in 1991 that they were quoted without permission and did not
advocate the views expressed in the book. Young and Martin Luther
King III have since become conspiracy supporters.

Saussy still thinks Ray was innocent.

"He [Ray] was not up to an assassination," said Saussy. "I'm sure
if he had sniffed murder in the errands he was running he would have
run the other way. He just didn't want trouble."

And if he is wrong?

"Then I've been conned," he said. "No man's opinions are infallible."

From the opening page of *The Tennessee Waltz*, it is clear that Ray didn't write it. It begins with a quotation from Henry David Thoreau's *Walden* that reads in part, "Wherever a man goes, men will pursue and paw him with their dirty institutions, and, if they can, constrain him to belong to their desperate odd-fellow society." It ends with the radical/biblical injunction, "Remember my bonds."

The book was self-published by Saussy and timed to coincide with the 20th anniversary of the King assassination. For a number of reasons it received little attention. Ray was then in robust health. Being a fugitive, Saussy could not exactly embark on a promotional tour. The King family had not endorsed the book as they did the later *Orders to Kill* by William Pepper. And the conspiracy fires had not been fanned as furiously as they were this year when the 30th anniversary coincided with Ray's death.

But the book contains the gist of the currently popular anti-government King-assassination conspiracies. *The Tennessee Waltz* is part Ray biography, part anti-government and anti-Nashville-establishment screed, and part radical Christian theology. Its subtitle is "The Making of a Political Prisoner," and it includes an 18-page afterword called "The Politics of Witchcraft," for which Saussy does claim full authorship.

"I didn't make a hard effort to find Saussy," said author Posner, whose book *Killing the Dream* was released in 1998. "I never had a chance to pursue it."

Posner said it is "absolutely" clear that Ray did not actually write *The Tennessee Waltz*, but he was unable to develop the Saussy angle because he was under a publisher's deadline to get the book out in time for the 30th anniversary.

The omission is a serious one in a book that purports to present the definitive portrait of James Earl Ray and debunk once and for all King assassination conspiracies. The bogus authorship makes Ray appear far smarter, more disciplined, and more intellectual than the manipulative con artist, holdup man, and jailhouse letter writer he was. And Saussy is key to understanding Ray's later affinity with attorney/publicist William Pepper and the peculiar assortment of clergymen who attached themselves to Ray's claim of innocence.

Posner attributed "anti-U.S. government leanings" to Ray, citing a critique of American policy toward Soviet defectors and deserters after World War II. Ray, he said, was "quite political on subjects ranging from Allied war crimes to alleged government cover-ups of dirty programs." This claim is fatuous. Saussy likely projected his own well-documented anti-government leanings and his deeper reading of history onto Ray.

His stint as Ray's ghostwriter and alter ego was not the first time Frederick Tupper Saussy had become, if not another persona, at least a very different person.

He was a 1958 graduate of the University of the South in Sewanee, where his fraternity brother, Patrick Anderson, remembered him as one of the most popular boys on campus, a musician, and cartoonist for the campus paper. His first job was as a prep-school teacher at Montgomery Bell Academy in Nashville. He married a teenager named Lola Haun, a Fifties girl with looks, family money, and a Corvette. Anderson, now a novelist in Washington, D.C., remembers it as a huge wedding with endless parties given by the most famous people in town.

The couple had two children and a house on posh Belle Meade Boulevard. Saussy became a successful advertising copywriter, known for his clever jingles and eccentricity. He and his wife had a pet monkey they named Thelonious Monk.

"He came and charmed Nashville," recalled author David Halberstam, who knew Saussy when Halberstam worked for *The Tennessean* in the early 1960s. "He played the piano and married a beautiful woman. They were the golden couple. Everything seemed to be his."

A talented jazz musician, Saussy began to concentrate on songwriting. He had a minor hit, "Morning Girl," which was nominated for a Grammy, and wrote other songs performed by the Nashville Symphony, Chet Atkins, Perry Como, Ray Stevens, and others. But the marriage ended in 1972, the songwriting career stalled, and the clever wordsmith who penned corny jingles for Purity Dairy turned his attention and skills to more serious matters. It was at about that time that Saussy was audited by the IRS. When Anderson ran into his old friend in the mid-Seventies, all Saussy wanted to talk about was taxes and the monetary system.

"I think it's tragic he got off on this political kick," said Anderson. "He is, in my opinion, a totally non-political person. He was living in a fantasy world. I don't think he had any sense of what he was doing or what the consequences could be."

In 1976, Saussy and his second wife and their 2-year-old son moved to Sewanee, seeking an idyllic, protected life on the mountaintop. He made money doing advertising and selling his watercolors. And he became enamored of Irwin Schiff, whose book *The Biggest Con* was something of a bible of the tax movement. Saussy would become, by turns, a self-styled theologian, restaurant owner, Ray's ghostwriter, King assassination conspiracy theorist, anti-government pamphleteer, and radical opponent of the federal government's taxation and monetary authority.

Saussy was convicted on only one count of failure to file tax returns. But he drew attention to himself with his courtroom antics and his outspokenness, prompting U.S. District Judge Thomas Hull to tell him, "You're so intelligent it hurts you."

His life as a fugitive apparently also had its share of surprising and colorful twists and turns. His flight was supported, if not assisted, by Jim Garrison, the late New Orleans prosecutor and famous JFK assassination conspiracy theorist. "Blowing about as the spirit led me" and going by various aliases, Saussy spent time as a religious counselor, pianist, computer handy man, homeless person, Bible student, and patron of public and university libraries from Seattle to Key West to Nashville. He played piano in various nightclubs. Five years ago he abandoned the hairpiece he was wearing as a disguise and began living a relatively normal life with his third wife, Nancy, in Southern California. Some of the people who cared for him knew his identity; others did not. One of those who did was a fellow fugitive who got caught and gave federal agents information that led to Saussy's capture.

"It was not the miserable existence one's imagination is prone to depict," he said. "I was never without a keyboard or music. If you had walked through Rainier Center Mall in Seattle's downtown during the summer of 1988, you'd have seen me playing Bach's Goldberg Variations on the Steinway grand that sits in the atrium."

When he was captured he was on his way to a quiet lunch with his 20-year-old son, an aspiring art student at Santa Monica City College. On a cool, rainy day, he opened the door to his garage, got in his car, and began to drive away when two cars suddenly blocked him in. A federal marshal got out, held up a badge, and asked if he was Frederick Tupper Saussy.

No, Saussy replied, he was not.

"That name had not been uttered for 10 years," Saussy explained. "I had become another persona. But he had some science that could disprove that."

He first spent several months in lockdown in Atlanta, where he passed time writing and reading the Bible while in virtual solitary confinement. At Taft, a low-security prison near Los Angeles, he is choir director and unofficial inmate counselor and prison minister. He will probably have to serve a total of about 20 months.

"Tupper had to come back at some time," Saussy said. "I'm spending my time productively. It's a marvelous experience. The fields are ripe for harvest and there is a lot of harvesting going on."

He was delighted to find a piano in the chapel at Taft, and has been giving voice, composition, and piano lessons to several promising inmates. One of the worst things about Atlanta, he said, was that he had to go five months without playing the piano, the longest such stretch in his life. He has not necessarily changed his views on government but seems to be planning a law-abiding life when he gets out of prison. If he is not exactly repentant about his pre-fugitive days, he does have misgivings about butting heads with federal authority.

"I had been reduced to an angry, frustrated voice that had no hope of ever being clearly brokered through channels of information most people trusted," he said. "Worse, I was beginning to discover that my approach was all wrong."

He is something of a hero to a few old friends, a con artist to others. Rusty Leonard, an attorney in Winchester and resident of Sewanee, said his involvement in one of Saussy's tax schemes cost both him and his father dearly. Leonard's father, a physician, went to prison for filing Fifth Amendment tax returns. The younger Leonard pled guilty to a single misdemeanor count of failing to collect taxes on his former business.

"Tupper pointed us in the direction and let us make our own mistakes," Leonard said. "I got myself in my own mess. My criticism of Tupper is that his entire motivation was in his pocketbook, either making money off what he was doing or taking advantage of someone. He's a brilliant man, but he did hurt a lot of people."

Last December, when Saussy returned to Chattanooga for sentencing, he briefly passed by some reporters. He smiled at them and said, "I believe in happy endings."

After half a year in prison, he thinks he has found it, even if it is not exactly the one he once seemed destined to enjoy.

"I want the government to get its pound of flesh," he said. "And I want to be safe behind my shield of Christian faith."

Double Exposure:
A Conspiracy Theory Unravels
(The Memphis Flyer, 1997)

James Earl Ray

A second theory embraced by lawyer/author William Pepper, The Commercial Appeal *and members of the King family claims that Army intelligence officers were desperate to stop King and stationed eight Green Berets in Memphis on April 4, 1968, to carry out a secret mission. One of the Green Berets named by Pepper, Billy Ray Eidson, won an $11 million libel judgment against Pepper and his publishers in 2000.*

Conspiracy theories involving governmental authorities in Memphis cannot be dismissed out of hand. If any reminder was needed, consider the case of former Shelby County Medical Examiner Dr. O. C. Smith. In 2002, Smith was purportedly attacked outside his office by an assailant who wrapped him in barbed wire, strapped a bomb around his neck, and chained him to a window grate. After an investigation that lasted more than a year, Smith was charged in a federal indictment with lying about the incident. He pleaded innocent and was awaiting trial in 2004.

Double Exposure:
A Conspiracy Theory Unravels

I t is the fantasy of many a newspaper reporter: Being interviewed
on prime-time national television about your big story.

Steve Tompkins, a former reporter for *The Commercial Appeal*,
found himself in that position in 1997 on the ABC program *Turning
Point*. The subject matter was nothing less than the biggest Memphis
news story of the century. The segment was titled "Who Killed Martin
Luther King?"

Tompkins talked with correspondent and *Nightline* host Forrest
Sawyer about his 1993 story about the Army spying on King, and the
newspaper itself was displayed for millions of viewers across the country.

Trouble is, Sawyer and ABC proceeded to blast holes in a
conspiracy theory founded on Tompkins' reporting, and raise serious
doubts about the accuracy of key — and unattributed — assertions in
the CA's story: to wit, that the Army's intelligence system was "desperately searching for a way to stop (King)" and that eight Green Berets
were in Memphis "carrying out an unknown mission" when King was
killed.

Tompkins wound up backpedaling from his conspiracy collabo-
rator, Dr. William Pepper, attorney for James Earl Ray and author of
the now discredited *Orders to Kill: The Truth Behind the Murder of
Martin Luther King*. He also disavowed an affidavit he signed vouching
for the accuracy of sections of Pepper's book.

The fiasco has infuriated Green Berets who are fighting mad and

determined to defend their reputation. It has left the *CA* doing some
fancy footwork and fresh reporting of the King "conspiracy," although
the newspaper and Tompkins stand by their story.

"We still stand by it," said *CA* managing editor Henry Stokes. "I
thought it was a good story, and it got a lot of attention nationally."

To be sure, the *CA* stopped short of Pepper's sensational claims.
He alleges that Ray is innocent and that Green Beret snipers with the
20th Special Forces Group were literally peering down the barrels of
their rifles at King and Andrew Young when King was shot, although
the fatal shot came from someone else. Pepper also claims the Army
officer who ordered the King hit was dead or killed. *Turning Point*
produced the man, very much alive and ornery, on camera, and icily
refusing to shake Pepper's hand.

Other Green Berets and Army officers connected to the 20th
Special Forces Group, including a Congressional Medal of Honor
winner, also deny that Green Berets were even in Memphis when King
was killed, as both Pepper and the *CA* claim.

"Steve just played with the wrong guys, and so did Mr. Pepper,"
said Rudi Gresham, an advisory board member of an organization of
Green Berets called the Special Forces Association. Gresham has made
it a personal two-year crusade to defend the reputation of the Green
Berets against the allegations. He helped arrange the ABC interview
by rounding up military records and former members of the 20th
Special Forces Group, including the "dead" alleged hit team leader, a
former supply sergeant named Billy Ray Eidson.

The lone sources for the allegations about the 20th Special Forces
Group are Tompkins and two unidentified men he said were among
eight Green Berets in Memphis when King was killed. Pepper hired
Tompkins to reinterview his sources, but did not talk to them himself.

Tompkins, who left *The Commercial Appeal* shortly after his
King story was published, collaborated with Pepper on *Orders to Kill*.
Now that the story is unraveling, they are pointing fingers at each other.

"Pepper took my series and embellished the hell out of it,"
Tompkins said.

The same charge can be made about Tompkins' series. It took
solidly sourced reporting about the Army's spying on three generations of King's family and embellished it with innuendo, intrigue, and

unattributed charges. Its ambiguity invited speculation by readers and conspiracy theorists prepared to make claims the newspaper only hinted at. And foremost among them were Dr. William Pepper and the family of Martin Luther King.

On March 21, 1993, Tompkins' 6,274-word story ran across the top of the front page, headlined "Army Feared King, Secretly Watched Him." The story stopped short of flatly stating that the Army took part in the King assassination. "This newspaper's investigation uncovered no hard evidence that Army Intelligence played any role in King's assassination, although Army agents were in Memphis the day he was killed," the story said.

But there were sinister implications in the seventh and eighth paragraphs of the story and much of the subsequent 6,000 words.

"By then (March of 1968) the Army's intelligence system was keenly focused on King and desperately searching for a way to stop him," the story said. "On April 4, 1968, King was killed by a sniper's bullet at the Lorraine Motel in Memphis."

The most shocking assertions and sinister quotations in Tompkins' story were unattributed and, in newspaper parlance, "buried" near the end of the story. For example, Tompkins described "murky clandestine operations" involving Vietnam veterans in this unattributed quotation: "They couldn't let a lot of these crazy guys back into the states because they couldn't forget their training. Birmingham (20th Special Forces Group headquarters) became Saigon. The rural South was in-country, and at times things got out of hand."

Citing its unnamed sources, the CA claimed the 20th Special Forces Group used "Klan guys who hated niggers" as its intelligence network and that "Green Berets from the 20th often spied on King and other black Americans during the 1960s."

Finally, five paragraphs from the end of the story came this sensational, tantalizingly ambiguous claim, spiced with fresh military jargon: "Eight Green Beret soldiers from an 'Operation Detachment Alpha 184 Team' were also in Memphis carrying out an unknown mission" on April 4, 1968, the day King was killed.

The nature of the "unknown mission" was not explained. The statement was not confirmed, denied, or commented upon by any of the "several dozen" Army personnel the newspaper said were interviewed.

Had they been contacted, any number of them could have, at the least, pointed out that Alpha 184 did not exist in 1968, Gresham said. It was part of a 1960 Louisiana company.

The story simply ended with the fatal bullet "from a 30.06 rifle equipped with a scope," the arrest and guilty plea of "the man whose fingerprints were found on that type gun, James Earl Ray," and the White House heaving a sigh of relief at the "clear and significant decline in the number and severity of riots and disorders" in the summer of 1968. The murder weapon, of course, has been a prime focus of Pepper and other conspiracy theorists for almost 30 years. They allege that the rifle that was recovered was a "throwdown" used to frame Ray. Curiously, the *CA* story accepts as fact that the murder rifle was equipped with a scope, but leaves doubt that it was recovered or that Ray fired it.

Tompkins and Stokes stand by the claim that Green Berets were in Memphis April 3rd and 4th on what Tompkins calls a "reconnaissance" mission. "We didn't know anything beyond that," said Tompkins. Stokes points out that "everything a unit like that does is secretive" and said, "Steve interviewed some people that would lead us to believe some people from that unit were here."

Stokes added, "There is a large difference between surveillance and murder. I don't think we were ever able to bridge that. We may have added some more circumstances to the factual buffet that is out there."

Col. Lee Mize was senior military adviser to the 20th SFG in April, 1968. He is a Congressional Medal of Honor recipient (1953) for action in the Korean War and, Gresham said, "a legend among legends" in the military. He told ABC it was "impossible" that Green Berets from 20th SFG were in Memphis. He repeated that in an interview with the *Flyer* in more depth and with considerable heat. He called Tompkins and Pepper "two con men, they're both conning each other."

Mize said he has known Eidson since they were boys, and that Pepper "better hope he don't really feel like killing somebody." Gen. Henry Cobb, former commander of the 20th SFG, said there was "no way" they could have been in Memphis without his knowledge. Gresham called the claims about Green Berets "total nonsense."

It is their word and documentation, including rosters and morning reports, against Tompkins' unnamed sources. Pepper's affidavit which Tompkins signed said:

"I have read the material in Dr. Pepper's book about these interviews conducted by me, in which he refers to these soldiers who now live outside the United States as "Warren" and "Murphy" and confirm its accuracy."

Tompkins said Pepper sent him Chapter 30 of the book "which I understood was the only part where I was mentioned." The chapter titled "Orders to Kill" is the climax of the book and includes the information from "Murphy and Warren," the two anonymous sources. Tompkins said he "skimmed" the book material, signed the affidavit, and told Pepper to "make sure you send me the final version of the book, which he never did."

The *CA* did not mention Eidson or Mize, nor did it print an apparently bogus set of Army orders sending Green Berets to Memphis which Pepper reprints in his book. Tompkins said he knew the orders were bogus the first time he saw them because the date was April 30, 1968, which was after the assassination.

Despite that red flag, however, the newspaper had enough confidence in the unnamed sources to trust their claims about the Green Berets in the 20th Special Forces Group. The story drew a prompt and scathing response from Gen. William Yarborough, who was interviewed in it and described as "the Army's top spy." His long letter to the editor was printed in full under the headline "Army's 'spy' story mixes few facts with lots of fiction."

Yarborough wrote: "The end product is a piece of journalism that seems to fulfill the basic requirements for what is known to psychological warfare experts as "agit-prop" — propaganda aimed at the creation of discord, divisiveness and disharmony."

Tompkins resigned from the newspaper shortly thereafter. Publication of a big story often brings a reporter a sense of elation, but Tompkins was "burned out with journalism." Stokes was supportive and sympathetic. "The kind of stuff he was doing is terrifically difficult to maintain year after year," he said. "It eats on you."

Tompkins and Pepper crossed paths in 1993.

"Bill came to see me in the fall of 1993," said Tompkins. "He wanted to talk to my sources in Washington, and later he asked me to take questions to members of the Green Beret team. I agreed to take some questions to one of my principle sources."

Pepper paid Tompkins. But both Tompkins and Stokes say the *CA* did not pay any sources. *On Turning Point,* Eidson angrily suggests that someone was paid to malign him.

In 1993, Pepper was in Memphis for the filming of a made-for-television mock trial of James Earl Ray. At a news conference then, Pepper said he had represented Ray for free since 1986. The prosecutor in the mock trial was former U.S. Attorney Hickman Ewing Jr. The mock jury acquitted Ray.

Pepper's book was published in 1995. Pepper wrote, "I reserve a special note of thanks for former Memphis journalist Steve Tompkins, whose earlier work opened the door to the most sensitive, deeply hidden area of my investigation. For me Steve epitomizes the very best of a dying breed in America — the investigative journalist who is only restricted in the pursuit of truth by his conscience."

To Jimmy Dean, administrator of the Special Forces Association in Fayetteville, N.C., the *CA*'s 1993 story had been an annoyance, but he did not get overly exercised about it. No Green Berets were named, the allegations were blunted, and it is difficult and time-consuming to disprove something by establishing the whereabouts of a lot of people 25 years ago. And there was Yarborough's letter.

Pepper's book was another matter. Dean directed an investigation of its charges beginning in 1995, with Gresham as his investigator. Sales were slow, but the book was advertised prominently in *The New York Times* under the blurb "Did The U.S. Army Order King's Death?" Later, Pepper was interviewed on CNN by Larry King. And the Martin Luther King family embraced the book.

"I never lighten up," said Gresham. "I became Mr. Pepper's worst nightmare."

He contacted Mize in Alabama, who told him Billy Ray Eidson was alive and well and came to see him two or three times a year. He reached Cobb, who had never heard of the book or Pepper. Meanwhile, ABC was working on a story about Pepper's book and urging Gresham to cooperate. With the help of Mize and Eidson's daughter, Gresham reached Eidson in Costa Rica. Eidson said he had never been to Memphis in his life.

"He laughed the first day," said Gresham. "The second day he was mad. And the third day it really sunk in that the King family believes he was involved in killing their daddy."

Eidson agreed to go to New York with Gresham, Mize, Cobb, and Dean to appear on *Turning Point*. Since the program aired, the *CA* has been coy in its own pages about the Tompkins-Pepper connection. In a front-page story it reported that the program "exposes flaws in Pepper's assertion that an Army Special Forces unit was stalking King in Memphis the day of the assassination." A later Metro section story more fully reported the denials that Green Berets were in Memphis at all. But there was no editorial retraction.

"Stalking" is not the same as "watching." Pepper clearly went further than the *CA* did with Tompkins' reporting. But they agree about this crucial point: Decorated Army officers directly involved with the Green Berets and the 20th Special Forces Group were and still are lying or ignorant about their colleagues' surveillance of Martin Luther King on several different dates and places including Memphis on April 4, 1968.

Jacqueline Smith
Keeps Watch at the Lorraine
(2004)

Jacqueline Smith

    The Lorraine Motel where Dr. King was killed is now the National Civil Rights Museum. Protester Jacqueline Smith has become as much a part of it as any exhibit because she has lived on the sidewalk across the street from the entrance since 1987. Few people, myself included, expected her to last that long when I first told her story weeks before she was evicted from the Lorraine.

Jacqueline Smith
Keeps Watch at the Lorraine

Sixteen years and 147 days. Six-thousand days by the summer of 2004. That's how long sidewalk protester Jacqueline Smith has carried on her vigil outside the National Civil Rights Museum, which used to be the Lorraine Motel, where Dr. Martin Luther King Jr. was assassinated in 1968.

The people who run the museum may not like it, but Smith has become as much a part of the museum as any exhibit. What's more, she's the ultimate interactive display, talking to thousands of visitors every year after year after year.

Jacqueline Smith had a dream deferred. Once she was a promising contralto who auditioned for the Metropolitan Opera and studied French and acting. At Douglass High School, class of 1969, she was president of the student council. Her gift was for singing. One of her instructors, Robert Kirkham, recalled her as a quiet, honest, independent young woman and "a grade-A operatic contralto." Alice Bingham, gallery owner and arts patron, helped the shy, skinny girl with glasses get a foundation award and an audition for the Met. "Out came this deep, contralto voice and we all just about died," she said.

Bingham helped Smith get a scholarship to the University of Southern Mississippi. But when it came time to enroll, Smith didn't show up. She took accounting courses at State Tech and worked at Sears for two years. Then she went to Chicago to sing with an opera company. It didn't work out for her there. Like all performers, she had her share of setbacks. But something was missing, maybe the great talent or maybe the encouragement and support to carry on in spite of disappointment. Kirkham said that "somewhere along the road she was confronted with that brick wall."

She went to work at the Lorraine in 1978. The motel's owner gave her a room and board. For six years a room on the second floor was her home. She made about $50 a week cleaning rooms and giving tours of the little shrine to King. She owned little other than second-hand dresses that she wore for King ceremonies and a color television she purchased from a rental agency for $15 a month. She has the slim, delicate features of a television anchor woman, but the dress is a hand-me-down from her mother and the earrings are imitation diamonds she bought for $10. Sometimes, she said, the men who come to the Lorraine got the wrong idea.

"I set them straight in a nice way. You tell them in a nice way you are not available."

She didn't turn them away. The Lorraine, she said, did not rent rooms to prostitutes. But it did rent to men who wanted a motel room for $20 at 10 in the morning or 3 in the afternoon. "We need the business," she reasoned. "It's not my business what they do as long as they pay the rent and sign the card. I'm not the police. It's not my jurisdiction to tell the girls what to do. I can't say get off the street. I respect them and they respect me. It's not for me to judge anyone. I don't mess with their trade or their tricks. I receive no cuts, never have. Prostitution didn't happen here overnight. It's been going on the last 20 years. The city is partly responsible. I've seen plenty of white men drive by here in cabs and take them away by the carload."

"If we didn't have a few loyal friends and customers and if it wasn't for the prostitutes and their efforts, then the Lorraine might well have been sold and bulldozed years ago," she said in 1987. "After 1968 business vanished. The Chisca Hotel closed. The Peabody closed. We stayed open. We get no help from the Lorraine Foundation. You see the clientele. We need money to run here. All the big money turned their back on us. So we went where the money took us. There is good here. I'm here. The owner, Mr. Bailey, is here. His brother is here. The Church of God in Christ had 14 rooms on reservation for their convention."

She reached in a drawer and pulled out a stack of receipts from convention members. Then she proudly displayed a scrapbook of thank-you letters from schoolchildren she escorted through King's room. There are pages and pages of Smith and visiting celebrities. The moments of shared stardom help compensate for her own humble surroundings.

"In a singing career, you survive off a little of nothing," she said with a shrug. "I meet all types of stars and celebrities, and you can't measure that with money. The main thing is, the hotel is still open."

That was 1987. But the hotel wasn't open much longer. A year later it closed and on March 2, 1988, Smith was evicted, dragged kicking and screaming on to the street along with a few possessions. And, with a modest concession to the courts and the museum of moving half a block away from the main entrance, that is where she has been ever since.

Smith has strong opinions and is not shy about expressing them. She has her own protest website and over the years has been an occasional caller to WHBQ talk radio, usually sounding off about the Civil Rights Museum, Beale Street, or gentrification of downtown. The Civil Right Museum, she believes, is "Exploiting the Legacy" of Dr. King, according to one of her banners, behind which she sits under the shade of an umbrella.

She is often asked how long she plans to stay on the sidewalk. She produces a card with a picture of King on one page and a picture of herself and her sidewalk living quarters on another and points at the text on the back.

"As long as I can make my message heard," it said, "I will carry on."

IV.
School Desegregation

Innocence and Integration

(Memphis, 1996; The Memphis Flyer, 2004)

The Memphis 13

Partly because it was non-violent, the desegregation of Memphis public schools beginning in 1961 received less attention than the desegregation of schools and public facilities in Little Rock, Nashville, and in Mississippi. But the story is no less important. The Memphis integration brigade of 1961 consisted of 13 brave first-graders. The Memphis lawsuit that set the events in motion was filed by Thurgood Marshall, who also argued Brown vs. Board of Education for the NAACP in 1954 and later served on the U.S. Supreme Court as the first black justice.

As Marshall once wrote, integration "with all deliberate speed" meant "slow" in the Deep South. It was left to the federal courts to speed up desegregation of the Memphis City Schools by court-ordered busing. The judge most closely identified with busing in Memphis, U.S. District Judge Robert McRae, died in 2004 at the age of 82.

Innocence and Integration

On a Memphis summer morning in 1971, 17 years after the highest court in the land outlawed segregation, the mayor of Memphis, Henry Loeb, pulled up to the intersection of Poplar and Third, glanced out his window, and saw the familiar face of U.S. District Judge Robert S. McRae.

Loeb, who was on the passenger side next to his plainclothes policeman driver, rolled down the window, looked at McRae and hollered, "Hey, you son-of-a-bitch, quit integratin' those schools," then grinned his famous grin and sped away.

The mayor pretty much expressed the sentiments of the majority of his white constituents at that time. But Judge McRae wasn't about to quit integratin' those schools. In fact, he had barely begun.

The next year, McRae ordered desegregation Plan A to bus 13,389 students. A year later, he followed it up with Plan Z, which called for the busing of nearly 40,000 students. Those students and their schools would knock down the walls of segregation.

The issue of busing dominated the political and social life of Memphis during the 1970s and well into the next decade. Busing was not unique to Memphis, of course. In city after city in both the North and South, federal courts called upon local school boards to use their public school systems as battering rams for integration.

With an evident eye to the future, the courts' chosen method involved children. Other approaches that might have focused upon adults, such as the use of property-tax rebates to encourage integrated neighborhoods, were put aside. The American dream of the melting pot and equal opportunity was set against the American dream of choosing a home and raising a family in a nice neighborhood with good schools.

It was no contest. Tens of thousands of white Memphians — some racist, many not — fled the city for points north, south, and east. Looking back, it is difficult to imagine anything that the most powerful suburban real estate developers and politicians in town could have concocted that would have done more to accelerate the growth of the county and the decline of the city of Memphis and its public schools.

Plan Z failed for a lot of reasons, but perhaps the main one is that people cannot be denied the right to vote with their feet. And Memphis and Shelby County — with its peculiar geography, two-headed government, separate school systems, and powerful churches — gave them options ranging from private schools to county schools to Mississippi schools just minutes away.

One of the more prophetic statements in the massive court record of *Northcross v. Memphis Board of Education*, the original Memphis schools desegregation case, was made by Federal Appeals Court Judge Paul C. Weick. In 1972, the Appeals Court upheld Memphis' first court-ordered busing plan, called Plan A, on a 2-1 vote. Weick dissented.

"The average American couple who are raising their children scrape and save money to buy a home in a nice residential neighborhood near a public school," he wrote. "One can imagine their frustration when they find their plans have been destroyed by the judgment of federal courts . . . The burden of eliminating all the ills of society should not be placed on public school systems and innocent school children."

Busing didn't create the suburbs, of course. It accelerated a process that was already well underway. From 1950 to 1970, the white population of Memphis had decreased by 2 percent while the black population had increased by 2 percent, according to census reports. The decline of the white population would have been much greater had it not been for the annexation of parts of East Memphis, Frayser, Parkway Village, and Oakhaven during that time.

But busing came at a time when Federal Express was on the verge of creating thousands of new jobs at the airport, when developers like Boyle Investment were building suburban office complexes, and when governments were building the roads to get people to the far reaches of Shelby County.

What was lost more than anything else was something best described as "connectedness" for want of a better word. Connectedness is the difference between a geographic area and a neighborhood, between school attendance and school spirit, and between a group of people and a caring community. Memphis hurts for connectedness, and busing is partly to blame.

Three decades after the onset of busing and 50 years after the U.S. Supreme Court's landmark ruling in *Brown v. Board of Education of Topeka*, Memphis and Shelby County were still dealing with the issues of desegregation and resegregation. The majority of schools in the city system are at least 95 percent black, and the number of white students in the system (9,239) declines by about 1,000 every year. The demand for new schools in the growing county school system has a direct impact on both city and county taxes because the school funding formula mandates that roughly $3 be spent on city school construction for every $1 spent on county schools.

As the country marked the 50th anniversary of the Brown decision, it had almost become a cliche to say that urban public school systems have returned to separate but equal, or "separate and unequal." But the self-segregation of Memphis and other school systems is not the same as legal segregation. Memphis has an open enrollment policy, all schools are air-conditioned, some inner-city schools are newer and better equipped than suburban schools, and the faculty is integrated. A look back at the Memphis schools in the Fifties and Sixties through the eyes of the students and parents who integrated them shows a very different world of unequal opportunity, segregated faculty, dilapidated buildings, fourth-hand textbooks, cruelty and discrimination.

In a follow-up to the Brown decision, the Supreme Court said schools must be integrated with "all deliberate speed." In Memphis and the states of the Deep South, "all deliberate speed" meant slow. The NAACP's Legal Defense Fund, organized by Thurgood Marshall in 1946, told NAACP branches to file petitions with school boards and, if no action was taken, to follow up with lawsuits. In 1960, there were still no black students in mixed schools in Mississippi, Alabama, South Carolina, Georgia, and Louisiana.

In 1958, 8-year-old Gerald E. Young tried to enroll at all-white Vollentine Elementary in Memphis but was turned away by the attendance officer, the assistant superintendent, and finally the superintendent and school board. The board was composed of what used to be called "leading citizens" including attorneys Walter P. Armstrong and John T. Shea, schools administration building namesake Frances E. Coe, Jane S. Seessel of the grocery store family, and Wells Fargo Armored Car Services chairman Julian B. Bondurant. They were backed by the mayor and the opinions and delaying tactics of U.S. District Judge Marion Boyd whose response was typical of federal judges in the South.

"The Supreme Court's decree (in *Brown II*) seemed to encourage the Southern states to design an almost endless series of plans designed to thwart desegregation," wrote author Roger Goldman in *Thurgood Marshall, Justice for All.*

In 1960, the Legal Defense Fund filed a lawsuit, *Northcross v. Memphis Board of Education.* Dr. T. W. Northcross was a Memphis dentist whose daughter Deborah was 8 years old. He was on the executive committee of the NAACP and an independent businessman who could handle reprisals better than others. At the time there were 53,142 white children and 42,061 black children in the system, all attending segregated schools.

"You have to remember where we were coming from," said former Memphis NAACP Executive Secretary Maxine Smith. "In the years after Brown, absolutely nothing was done here to integrate our schools. They started building all-black schools like Carver and Lester near white neighborhoods just to keep them out of schools like Southside and East. It was shameful."

Smith, married to prominent dentist and former Shelby County Commissioner Dr. Vasco Smith, has bitter memories of the late Fifties in Memphis. "I would go down to court and listen to them lie about how our schools weren't segregated and watch U.S. District Judge Marion Boyd nod his head and agree. I was mortified. There was so much resistance, so much resistance."

But Northcross, the Smiths, and other Memphis NAACP leaders were not cowed. On their side were two of the great lawyers of the civil rights era, Thurgood Marshall and Constance Baker Motley, described as a foe of segregation "tougher than Grant at Vicksburg." When the schools were integrated in 1961, the most difficult challenge for the NAACP was persuading black parents to let their children be used as pioneers. The violent integration of Little Rock's Central High School in 1957, which got news coverage around the world, was a vivid memory.

"I bet we went to 200 homes trying to get volunteers," Smith said. "It was difficult to persuade the mothers that this was good for their kids."

Compounding the problem, classes had already started when integration began that fall and students were enrolled in neighborhood schools with their friends. And in the cruelest stroke of all, the desegregation plan called for integrating one grade at a time, starting with the first grade.

The iconic photographs of the civil rights era documenting school desegregation show Autherine Lucy being pelted with rocks and eggs by students at the University of Alabama in 1956; Elizabeth Eckford hugging her books to her chest while a mob of screaming white women harass her as she walks alone to Central High in Little Rock in 1957; and James Meredith arm-in-arm with federal marshals trying to register him for classes at Ole Miss in 1962. By comparison, desegregation of the Memphis public schools was nonviolent, but the photographs stand out for another reason. The children were so little, just 5 and 6 years old, possibly the youngest and most innocent civil rights vanguard in the South. When they sat down to have their picture taken, their feet didn't touch the floor.

The 13 students whose parents eventually agreed to participate were assigned to four schools, with no more than four black students at any one school. The NAACP wanted them all to look sharp in their Sunday best, but in fact some of them were too poor to buy new shoes and wore borrowed clothes.

The Rev. Samuel "Billy" Kyles recalled taking his 6-year-old daughter Dwania to her first day of class at Bruce Elementary School in October of 1961.

"Some of the other parents of the 13 black children who were integrating the schools were getting uneasy and were going to pull out," he said. "Then Claude Armour, who was the police chief and a segregationist, told his officers, 'If you can't protect these little nigra children then you can turn in your badge and gun tonight.' I appreciated that."

Dwania Kyles said classmates asked to see her tail "because black people were supposed to have tails." Her art teacher called her work "unusual" because "she colors the faces of all characters brown" including Dick and Jane and Santa Claus.

For one student, the experience was especially painful. Michael Willis was assigned to Bruce along with Kyles and one other student who later transferred back to his old school. In pictures of the 13 students, Willis is the smallest one. His father, A. W. Willis Jr., was a well-known Memphis lawyer and co-counsel in the desegregation lawsuits.

Three months before the schools were desegregated, A. W. Willis Jr., made local news when he was named to the board of the Memphis Transit Authority only to be replaced days later by Loeb for being "extremist." Willis did not take it lying down. The afternoon newspaper, *The Memphis Press-Scimitar*, published a long statement by him in which he called Loeb a "racist dictator" bent on a "race terror campaign."

Two months later, Michael Willis was in the newspaper as one of the 13 students desegregating the schools. Making matters worse for him, the Willis family and their friends were reasonably well-to-do professionals at a time when many of the white students who went to Bruce lived in the Lamar Terrace public housing project. Little Michael came to school and was picked up in a Cadillac. He was, he recalled, not just "nigger." He was "rich nigger." He was called names, pushed down stairs, mocked at the water fountain about not being able to "get the brown off" and isolated by his teacher and classmates, with the exception of Kyles.

"I was already going to my neighborhood school two blocks from our house when I transferred to Bruce," said Willis, who changed his name in 1986 to Menelik Fombi. "A few people befriended you, but you might have a friend Monday through Thursday then on Friday they were not your friend. I really feel like the teacher did not like having me in her class. It was a very difficult year. I feel like I was always on the defensive.

"My parents were hellbent on keeping me there. Deep down inside, I wish it had not happened to me. I have three children myself, and going to first grade in a loving environment is so important. I was just not on a solid foundation. It made me more reserved as a person, more defensive, and never sure if I was doing the right thing."

For E. C. Marcel Freeman, the desegregation experience was not as traumatic. Now E. C. Fentress, she was one of four black students assigned to Rozelle Elementary School. Her mother, Mattie Freeman, was a civil rights activist whose three oldest children did not have the opportunity to attend integrated schools. When the doors of opportunity opened, she was determined that her fourth child would take advantage of it. Fentress has good memories of her first-grade and second-grade teachers.

"That opportunity to learn what other students were learning was magnificent," she said. "I can only guess that my experiences were different because I was quiet. I kind of stayed to myself."

She graduated from Hamilton High School and the University of Memphis with honors. She has been a fifth-grade and sixth-grade teacher at Coleman Elementary School since 1978. When she started, Coleman was approximately 40 percent black and 60 percent white. Now it has 620 black students and 14 whites. One of her students recently won a poster contest to commemorate the 50th anniversary of *Brown v. Board of Education.*

"We are a Title I school but the opportunities are there," she said. "We have laptops, library cards, science clubs. The integration process had to take place. That door had to be opened. We have open enrollment in city schools. If you apply yourself and qualify, I don't know any door that isn't open."

Deborah Northcross, namesake of the Memphis lawsuit, graduated from an integrated Central High School in 1969, went to college at Mount Holyoke, and is director of a program at the University of Tennessee Health Science Center that helps minority students enter the doctoral program. She is grateful to Central for giving her a good education, newer textbooks than the ones used by her friends at all-black schools, and a heavier homework load. But she feels whites then and now often got the wrong message.

"Desegregation gave whites the impression we wanted to be with them and that was not the point," she said. "It was a matter of school choice and educational equity."

The 12 years that Fombi, Kyles, and Freeman spent in the Memphis public schools from 1961 to 1973 spanned the major milestones of both desegregation and resegregation. The grade-a-year plan held for five years, then the pace of integration increased all across the country. Congress passed the Civil Rights Act of 1965. In 1966 the Memphis City Schools faculty was integrated, and all 12 grades were integrated, but often with only token numbers. By 1969, for example, East High School had 1,866 white students and 19 blacks. Nearby Lester Junior High and High School were all black.

Integration began in earnest with the Supreme Court's 1971 decision approving busing as a means of desegregation. Student enrollment reached an all-time high of 148,015 in 1970-71, making the Memphis City Schools system the tenth largest in the country. By 1973, all deliberate speed had become full speed ahead thanks to Desegregation Plans A and Z and Judge McRae.

In his retirement, McRae isolated himself in a carrel at the University of Memphis library and prepared a nine-part oral history for the university's Mississippi Valley Collection. He was surrounded by scrapbooks of newspaper clippings, court documents, boxes full of old hate mail, and a score of yellow legal pads on which he wrote outlines in longhand. His famous red judicial robe was replaced by casual clothes and an ever-present Greek fisherman's cap.

Did it work, a visitor asked?

"Yes it worked," he said. "People are going to debate that because they disagree on what the purpose was, but yes, it worked. The plan was to get rid of the biracial school system. It did. It wasn't part of the plan to run the whites off. They just left."

After Plan A ordered the busing of 13,789 students in 1973, approximately 8,000 white students left the system. A federal appeals court ruled that Plan A was "but a first step." Plan Z called for busing 39,904 students, although only 28,000 actually participated. Another 20,000 white students left the system. Within a year, Memphis had the largest white private school system in the country.

"I tried to stop with Plan A but the appeals court wouldn't allow that. I was disappointed in the reaction to Plan Z. But I had to keep a stiff upper lip because this (reaction) was an act of defiance. Still I was disappointed that we hadn't come up with something that had worked the way we planned it.

"No, I wouldn't do it any other way. I am convinced there was nobody who could have settled this the way the parties were opposed. Somewhere along the line I became convinced that it was morally right to desegregate the schools."

Maybe it was during his tenure as a state court judge in the 1960s, when black lawyers still couldn't use the local Bar Association library. Maybe it was his association with Memphis judge and NAACP leader Benjamin Hooks, who helped ease McRae's appointment to the federal bench in 1966. And maybe it had something to do with that smirking, cavalier, "Hey you son-of-a-bitch" salutation from the highest elected official in the city of Memphis. Whatever the turning point, by 1972 McRae was determined to desegregate the public schools, two of which (Snowden and Central) he had attended himself. Someone once introduced him by saying that Central had two famous graduates: Machine Gun Kelly and Robert McRae.

It is often overlooked that, for a variety of reasons, Plan Z was not popular with many blacks either. The NAACP wanted 60,000 students bused and unsuccessfully sued to overrule Plan Z, which it called "a grotesque distortion of the law." A total of 26 inner-city schools were never integrated, either because there were not enough white students to go around or because the architects of desegregation believed white students would refuse to attend them. Black parents complained to civil rights lawyers that marijuana, LSD, and other drugs were far more common at white schools like East than at black schools. Others were worried to the point of tears about putting their children on crosstown buses.

"Judge McRae was as easy on the school system and the city as he could possibly have been," said O. Z. Stephens, a former city schools official who helped devise the desegregation plan. "Plan A might have held the white population but we would not have had integration. It was something that had to be tried. There would have never been any rest in this city until it was tried. Plus, the Constitution said we had to."

So O. Z. Stephens wrote Plan Z.

The title was McRae's idea. After Plan A, he did not want to deal with a succession of Plans B, C, D, etc. So he dubbed the first acceptable plan Plan Z in hopes that it would prove to be the terminal plan. And, for the most part, it was.

"Inasmuch as my middle initial was Z, I got tagged with it," Stephens recalled years later. "My identification with Plan Z killed me professionally in the school system."

Still, he called McRae a profile in courage who could easily have ruled in favor of the school board, let the appellate court overrule him, and let them take the heat. His unsung hero of school desegregation is John P. Freeman, superintendent of Memphis City Schools for most of the 1970s.

"He was a big, tough, salty South Memphis railroader and product of the school system. He had been a navigator on a B-17 bomber in World War II and could be unbelievably profane but he had a big heart. He made Plan Z work. He was the one who went head to head with Mayor Wyeth Chandler over all the impediments. When the bus drivers threatened to walk out, he raged at them, 'You blankety-blanks will blankety-blank pick up those little kids.' And they did."

There was one at least partial school success story. Optional schools are magnet schools or schools within schools for college-bound students or students with special interest in theater or some other area. They are open to students from outside their attendance zone and include some of the most racially balanced schools in the city system. Started in the Seventies, optional schools such as Grahamwood and John P. Freeman, however, began to self-segregate by the late nineties. And there was a distillation effect that concentrated a high percentage of National Merit Scholars and other top academic students at White Station High School while effectively gutting other schools of their best and brightest, both black and white.

By the mid-nineties, the impact on school spirit and high school sports was obvious to teachers like Karen Champion, a Spanish teacher at Central High School and 1967 graduate of Hamilton High School.

"Our games were packed when I was at Hamilton," she said. "Now unless the team is great it's difficult to get fans. When kids don't live in the neighborhood and can't walk to games there is not as much loyalty to the school."

On the 50th anniversary of *Brown v. Board of Education*, white flight is very much an ongoing process. On average, 1,000 white students have left the city system each year for the last ten years. Memphis today has one of the 20 largest and most segregated school systems in the country. The enrollment of 115,461 students includes 101,232 blacks, 4,897 Asians and Hispanics, and 9,239 whites. The number of whites would be lower had the city system not absorbed four county schools with racially mixed enrollments in 1999. Ten years ago, there were nearly 20,000 whites in the city system. Explained another way, the chances are better than nine out of ten that a black student in Memphis attends a school that is at least 90 percent black enrollment. Nationally, only 38 percent of black students go to such schools.

The Shelby County School system has 47,042 students including 31,455 whites (67 percent), 1,461 Asians (3 percent), 1,270 Hispanics (3 percent), and 12,618 whites (27 percent). The trends that swept the Memphis schools in the Seventies and Eighties are now taking place in some county schools. Germantown High School, which was 65 percent white in 2001, is now 44 percent white. Southwind Elementary, which was 32 percent white in 2001, is 15 percent white this year.

One Germantown resident who knows a bit about the desegregation of city and county schools is attorney Louis Lucas. If busing was the battering ram to break down desegregation, Lucas was the legal mastermind who helped decide where, when, and how the blows would be struck.

He was a white graduate of Catholic schools and Tulane University in New Orleans. In the 1960s, his Southern accent sometimes made Northern liberals distrust him. And his girth and short stature belied his intellectual toughness. After working for the U.S. Attorney in New Orleans and the civil rights division of the Department of Justice in Washington, he moved to Memphis in 1967 to form the city's first integrated law firm with Russell Sugarmon, A. W. Willis Jr., and Marvin Ratner. For the next ten years, Lucas and a young long-haired Memphis attorney named William Caldwell, supported by the NAACP Legal Defense Fund, were the dynamic duo of school desegregation.

Lucas believed systematic segregation did not go away after the Jim Crow laws of *Plessy v. Ferguson* were struck down. It continued because of neighborhood patterns, which were influenced by bankers and realtors, and school attendance zones, which in Memphis were drawn for many years by a whites-only school board presided over by a realtor appointed by the mayor. He mocked desegregation prior to Plan Z as "would-you-believe-this-one" plans and the subsequent white flight to hastily established church-sponsored academies as "the enormous religious revival and construction boom."

In addition to Memphis, he argued desegregation cases in Detroit, Cincinnati, Dayton, Milwaukee and other cities. He made three appearances before the U.S. Supreme Court. On his office wall he displayed signed pictures from John F. Kennedy, J. Edgar Hoover, and former U.S. Attorney General Ramsey Clark. In short, Lucas was something of a civil rights superstar in his day.

"Plan Z eliminated a basic structure of white and black schools in large areas of the city," he said in 1996. "It left a block of schools untouched. But to say the whole plan was a failure is to ignore gains I think have been made in both perception and actual interaction of children in the schools. Memphis is no longer perceived as a white system in which blacks are allowed to attend certain schools."

Unlike his former colleague Caldwell, who moved to Alaska and worked for Legal Services, Lucas several years ago quit making his living trying to right society's wrongs. He was succeeded by another civil rights lawyer, Richard Fields. After 1978 Lucas served as general counsel for William B. Tanner, then established a business law practice. At the age of 60, he said he was "still an idealist but probably not as much." He raised his children in Germantown, where they attended Dogwood Elementary and Houston High School.

"My kids went to county schools because that is where we lived when we had children," he explained. "We didn't move out there for the schools."

Dogwood at the time had 15 blacks among its 994 students. Houston had 136 blacks out of a student body of 1,860. Under the old Memphis Board of Education scoring system, all 2,854 students attended integrated schools.

The irony of that did not appear to make Lucas uncomfortable. Asked if he would have let his daughters be bused to Kirby High School, which was 53 percent black in 1996, he said yes, he would. He was less definite about East High School, a city school which is almost all black. That would be "a pretty good ride," he noted. "It's what's at the end of the line that counts."

The question was hypothetical. Who can say how they would act in such a situation? How do you weigh the abstract ideal of racial integration against something as near and dear as the education and childhood of your own children?

In the real world, Lucas never had to do that. But anyone who lived in Memphis and raised children after 1973 did.

The Last Integrationist

(The Memphis Flyer, 2001*)*

Richard Fields

What we say and what we do are often two different things, especially when the subject is public education in a city such as Memphis. Both of my children attended Memphis City Schools and were in the optional program, magnet schools for college-bound students in a 118,000-student system that is 90 percent minority and leads the state every year in the number of failing schools. How my wife and I would have responded if faced with court-ordered busing and Desegregation Plan Z I can't say. Like thousands of other middle-class and affluent parents, we probably would have opted out if it weren't for optional schools. Moreover, every school board member and superintendent knows it, and that is one reason things are the way they are.

The enforcers of the desegregation plan were tough, skillful attorneys such as Richard Fields, along with the NAACP. The issue of equity in education has dominated the politics and population movements of Memphis and Shelby County for 50 years.

The Last Integrationist

Reporters and editors, newspapers and newsmakers, judges and bad guys, politicians and prosecutors — they come and go. Richard Fields endures.

For three decades as a civil rights lawyer, Fields has influenced the way Memphians hold elections, treat prisoners, educate children, allocate property taxes, build public housing, sell cars, promote firemen and run day-care centers.

Memphians like to talk about bridging the gap between the black and white communities. Fields is something of a human bridge.

He's a 56-year-old, California-born-and-bred, Stanford-educated sole practitioner who lives with a pet rooster in the historic Wright Carriage House in Victorian Village. His father was a winemaker. Fields favors jeans, cowboy boots, and loud open-necked shirts. He sports a gray beard and a ponytail. His fingerprints, and often his quotes, are all over scores of front-page stories. Raised as a Lutheran, he was one of the first white men in Memphis to be legally married to a black woman. The marriage didn't take. Neither did the next three.

Shown a partial list of cases over the years, Fields studied it for a moment, nodded, then put it down with a shrug: "I know a lot of people in Memphis."

He came here in 1969 to work for the Teacher Corps at Georgia Avenue Elementary, an inner-city school. It was the year after Martin Luther King Jr., was assassinated. Not a good time, for sure, but a time

of opportunity just the same, with liberals, blacks, and women coming
to the fore and making their marks.

Two events were formative.

First, he married a black woman at St. Thomas Catholic Church,
something taboo and even illegal in parts of the Old South. The marriage, he said, "gave me a different perspective than a lot of people."

Second, in the fall of 1969, black leaders organized "Black
Mondays" to press their demands for representation on the all-white
school board. More than 60,000 students and 600 teachers skipped
school. The only white teacher was Richard Fields. The only principal
was Willie Herenton.

It proved to be a good career move for both of them. Herenton
rose through the ranks to become superintendent with the support of
the Memphis NAACP, which insisted he get the job over a white
candidate favored by the school board. Fields left teaching for law
school at the University of Tennessee, then returned to Memphis in
1976 to work in an integrated civil rights law firm with the late
Marvin Ratner and Russell Sugarmon. He immediately began working
on high-profile school desegregation cases.

Jimmy Carter was elected president that year. One of the things
he did was appoint more black judges than his predecessors had. Blacks
were still a minority in Memphis, but by 1980 they could claim some
judgeships, school board seats, and the superintendent's job. It was a
good time and place for a young civil rights lawyer to start his career.

Through thick and thin, Fields hitched his wagon to Herenton's
star. They did not always agree. Fields was the unbending idealist,
Herenton the embattled pragmatist. One thing they split on was busing.

"When I was superintendent, I did not want segregated schools,
but we reached a point where in my opinion busing had run its
course," said Herenton. "My position was, 'Gentlemen, let's call a
truce. Busing has not worked.' Richard was adamant that I was trying
to return the public schools to segregation."

Fields was Herenton's personal attorney when he weathered a
scandal involving a relationship with a former teacher, Mahnaz
Bahrmand. When Herenton ran for mayor in 1991, Fields and Dr.
Harry Moore, a liberal preacher, were the only two prominent whites
to publicly support him. Herenton's 49-percent share of the vote

would have thrown him into a runoff but for a landmark federal court lawsuit pressed by Fields, the NAACP, and others and resolved that year.

"Dr. Herenton," he said, "has been absolutely a godsend to Memphis."

And to Richard Fields. Backing Herenton in 1991 was a little like investing in AOL at $10 a share. Herenton has been mayor for three terms and counting and shows no signs of giving up the job. Fields has been there to hold his coat. At various times, he has been the mayor's lawyer, political adviser, schools liaison, and spin master on issues ranging from the 1999 mayoral election to the firing of police officers to the NBA arena.

"My theory of law," Fields said, "is do as many cases as you can that involve the broadest impact."

What sets him apart from most lawyers is not only the range of his cases but his media connections. Approachable and savvy, he is often a source for reporters covering the federal courts or the school boards. What appears to be reportorial research is sometimes, on closer inspection, a repackaging of Fields' research, briefs, depositions, or the comments of his clients. In newspaper terminology, he can set the agenda sometimes merely by filing a lawsuit. For example, "Fired officer sues for $6 million" was the headline of a front-page story on Harold Hays and the sheriff's department in 1996. The attention grabbing number, as is often the case in such lawsuits, was window dressing. The lawsuit was settled for $650,000.

"I certainly don't control the media," said Fields. "I think I have credibility with the media but that is partly the nature of the cases. I'm not a self-promoter. I give the reporters facts and expect them to investigate fully."

Fields and the NAACP Legal Defense Fund have pressed the cause of desegregation of public schools from the inner-city to the most distant eastern reaches of Shelby County in Arlington, literally the last mile. He delayed construction of a new Arlington high school until satisfied that it would have a significant black population.

"They cannot build a $40 million all-white high school," he vowed. "That just ain't gonna happen."

He is often out of step with black politicians as well who favor rebuilding low-enrollment "neighborhood schools" such as Manassas

High school or Carver High School with all-black populations. Separate but equal is no problem for the city school system, at least financially. Under the county funding formula, city schools get nearly $2.50 for construction for every $1 spent on county schools.

Asked if he ever feels like the last integrationist, Fields pondered the question. "I don't know," he said finally. "I think everyone believes in integrated schools," while acknowledging that most affluent city leaders send their children to private schools or city optional schools.

Sometimes Fields is on the side of the angels. He handled a case for low-income homeowners against former assessor Michael Hooks and won more than $3 million but took no fee. In another case, he and associates won $9 million from Home Depot for 300 residents of the old McKinney Truse neighborhood that was leveled to make way for the store on Poplar in East Memphis. Their fee of nine percent over the ten years of finding the residents, keeping them together, and winning the lawsuit did not even cover their hourly billings.

In other cases, Fields can be a pain in the neck.

"A lot of my friends don't understand my friendship with Richard because he irritates the hell out of them," said Herenton.

Since 1993, he has won seven judgments and settlements against the Shelby County Jail and sheriff's office totaling $2.43 million, with others pending. His lawsuits against the Cherokee Day Care centers targeted both corruption and members of the politically powerful Ford family, Herenton's rivals. When Herenton ran against Joe Ford in 1999, Fields made sure the lawsuit got plenty of attention. And he used Black Monday-style tactics against automobile dealers Bud Davis Cadillac and Covington Pike Toyota on behalf of black employees. Unapologetic, Fields said fair is fair. The dealers, he claimed, launched their own "preemptive publicity" aimed at polishing their image.

Posing for a picture in his yard, Fields apologized to his guest and finally answered his beeping cell phone, speaking loudly in a stage voice. The Covington Pike story, it seemed, had attracted national attention. Memphis could be getting a visit from Jesse Jackson. Fields tucked the cell phone back in his pocket and grinned.

V.
The Disposable City and Suburban Sprawl

What the Proprietors
Saw in 1828
(The Memphis Flyer, 2004)

Front Street, Memphis

Memphis has no shortage of plans produced by thoughtful and high-priced consultants. But Memphis doesn't grow or build things according to plans. It's more of an outlaw city, where politics is rough and tumble, and the people who get something done as opposed to talking about doing something know how to use their elbows, and that has been true of Fred Smith, Harold Ford, C. H. Butcher Jr., Jackie Welch, Jack Belz, Henry Turley, Kristi and Dean Jernigan, Pitt Hyde, and Michael Heisley.

A section of downtown riverfront property called The Promenade was dedicated to public use by the founders of Memphis. The exact interpretation of "public use" is being hotly debated today in a way the founders would surely appreciate and understand.

What the Proprietors
Saw in 1828

With the convention center, trolley, and now the FedEx Forum almost finished, how strange that the next big proposed downtown project hinges on interpretation of a document written in 1828, when wild bears and Indians roamed the town.

The Riverfront Development Corporation (RDC) wants to remake downtown's front door or promenade by replacing some public buildings and parking garages with an apartment building and an office building up to 40 stories tall. Over half of the promenade would remain public park, sidewalks, or open space. A group called Friends of the Riverfront opposes the plan.

In 20 years of writing about downtown, I have heard numerous references to the city founders and "the heirs" and the founders' bequest that created the promenade between Front Street and the Mud Island parking garage. But until last week I had never looked at the original document itself or a copy of it. It was long past time to check the original sources.

So I visited the Shelby County Archives, where archivist John Dougan dug into the Shelby County Register's Office deed book of 1828 and produced a handwritten copy. The problem was that some of the writing was hard to decipher and some was illegible. A trip to the Memphis Room at the Central Library, however, turned up a transcription in J.M. Keating's *History of the City of Memphis and Shelby County*, published in 1888.

Memphis was founded in 1819 — a date that splits the difference between the appointment of commissioners for the Chickasaw Treaty in 1818 and the opening of a land office on the bluff in 1820. The names to remember are Overton, McLemore, and Winchester. John Overton was a judge. Marcus Winchester was the first mayor. And John McLemore was, according to historians, one of the most influential and enlightened men of his day. Together they were known as "the proprietors" of the land on which Memphis was founded.

What happened between 1819 and 1828 is relevant and instructive to what is happening today with the RDC and the riverfront.

Charles Crawford, professor of history at the University of Memphis, said the proprietors were "hardheaded, realistic businessmen." But they did a remarkable thing. They dedicated a web of squares, alleys, streets, and the promenade to public use while keeping the rights to operate a ferry or two at the waterfront.

Crawford agrees with Keating's judgment that "Up to that time (1820) no scheme, plan, or plat had ever been made for an American city on so generous a scale. Every emergency in the life of a leading commercial point was provided for."

So, did the early citizens of Memphis rise up in gratitude and call them blessed? No.

"The people of Memphis were opposed to the proprietors and did everything they could to hinder and hamper them," wrote Keating in 1888. One sore point was the promenade and access to the river. Someone cut a road through it to the river, then another, dividing the promenade into three parts.

In 1828, Judge Overton wrote a letter to William Lawrence and Winchester expressing his concern about the division of the promenade. He complained about the "great want of appreciation of the liberality of the proprietors in laying out the town" and suggested his critics were "stupid." Imagine a public official talking that way.

The proprietors, "having been informed that doubts have arisen in relation to their original intention," decided to restate their vision and file it in the record books. The language is a little cumbersome but worth quoting since it is likely to come up in public meetings, City Council sessions, and maybe even another court case:

"In relation to the piece of ground laid off and called the

'Promenade,' said proprietors say that it was their original intention, is now, and forever will be, that the same should be public ground for such use only as the word imports, to which heretofore, by their acts, for that purpose, it was conceived all right was relinquished for themselves, their heirs, etc., and it is hereby expressly declared, in conformity with such intention, that we for ourselves, heirs and assigns, forever relinquish all claims to the same piece of ground called the 'Promenade,' for the purpose above mentioned."

It was 1828. No one contemplated that bridges would some day be built across the river, much less the arenas and condominiums that followed.

Today, one thing Memphis arguably lacks is a skyline and Front Street worthy of its blufftop location. For better or worse, the vision of the proprietors is responsible for that.

Interstate 40 Stops Here

(Memphis, 1996)

Anyone who drives regularly between Nashville and Little Rock is well acquainted with Memphis traffic jams at the Interstate 40 bridge over the Mississippi River and at the eastern edge of the city. On hot summer days, Memphis may well be the most frequently cursed city in the South by those stuck in such traffic jams. The fact that the interstate goes around and not through the city is due to an epic legal battle in the Sixties and Seventies that reached the U.S. Supreme Court. In the spring of 2004, the never-used Midtown expressway ramps on Interstate 40/240 were dismantled, 30 years after they were built.

Interstate 40 Stops Here

Citizen activism came of age in the 25-year battle to keep a six-lane interstate highway from going through Overton Park. Like the Civil War, the fight set neighbor against neighbor, family members against each other, and left physical and emotional scars on the city that remain to this day. The debate reached the United States Supreme Court and attracted national attention for several years. The unfinished 3.8 mile link through Midtown had the distinction of being the only break in Interstate 40 from North Carolina to California, until the northern loop of the interstate around Memphis was rechristened I-40.

Today that land has been redeveloped with new homes built to historic guidelines replacing the ones that were bulldozed in the 1960s and 1970s. The decision that made this possible was signed on January 16, 1981. On that date Federal Highway Administrator John Hassell declared that "this segment of Interstate Route 40 is not essential to the completion of a unified and connected interstate system."

That was the official death notice for the road. But killing it had taken the combined efforts of citizen activists, the Supreme Court, the conservation movement, Congress, and a young Memphis attorney named Charles Newman. Farsighted Memphians were talking up an east-west road through Overton Park as early as 1955, a full year before Congress and President Eisenhower established the National Interstate and Defense Highway System. Some were alarmed by the specter of suburban shopping malls. Already Poplar Plaza was eating into the profits of downtown businesses. It had not yet been demonstrated, of course, that highways could just as easily take people away from a city as bring them into it. In early 1957, a map of the proposed road through the park was published in the newspapers, and by the end of the year road opponents had formed the Committee for the Preservation of Overton Park. It's part of local mythology that a group of little old ladies in tennis shoes stopped the expressway, and there is some truth to this. Opponents were easy to caricature when they talked about disruption of the sex lives of the raccoons in the park.

But underestimating them was a fatal mistake. An activist named Anona Stoner was especially dedicated, savvy, and battle-tested. She came to Memphis in 1962 from Ohio, where she had led a fight to stop a highway from going through a park and Antioch College. Her key contribution was persuading road opponents that they should stop talking about saving midtown neighborhoods and instead focus on the park. That would ultimately turn a local issue into a national one. Grassroots opposition in Memphis would be bolstered by the financial resources of the Sierra Club and the Audubon Society and the legal protections of the federal parklands statutes.

By 1969, were ready to sue but they couldn't find a Memphis lawyer to take the case. Finally Stoner found one in Washington D.C., John Vardaman. Newman, who was with the Memphis firm Burch Porter & Johnson, later came aboard as local counsel. Citizens to Preserve Overton Park v. Secretary John Volpe was filed in 1969 in Washington and transferred to Memphis. It reached the U.S. Supreme Court in 1971. In an opinion written by Thurgood Marshall, the court said the parklands statutes were "plain and explicit." Federal funds could not be used to build a highway through a park unless there were no "feasible and prudent" alternatives.

Important as that ruling was, the issue was still very much alive. "One of our main points was that the state failed to take the first step toward compliance with the law," said Newman. "They would set up straw-man alternatives and then knock them down. The land had already been taken, the houses bulldozed. I think that was part of the state's strategy, and I know it influenced the thinking of some key people."

Many of the city's most powerful citizens including Peabody hotel developer Jack Belz and banker Ron Terry believed it would be a terrible mistake not to finish the road. The Memphis City Council, City Beautiful, the NAACP, and other organizations were for it. The trucking industry called delays "highway robbery" and "environmental tyranny." In 1976, U.S. Senator Bill Brock vowed to "get out there myself with a pick and shovel."

By 1978, however, the Chamber of Commerce, Future Memphis, the two daily newspapers, and the city and county mayors had grudgingly agreed that alternatives should be seriously studied. A delegation including Newman, Palmer Brown of the chamber, and Neely Mallory of Future Memphis tried to get an audience with then-governor Ray Blanton. He refused to see them. Finally, a Memphis political crony arranged the meeting. In a vintage performance, Blanton crudely lambasted everyone in the room before they could say a word and made it clear he would not give an inch. "I don't think he ever really got it straight who was on which side," Brown said.

Two more years passed before Memphis Mayor Wyeth Chandler wrote Governor Lamar Alexander that "we are utterly convinced that to continue further attempts . . . would be futile." Two weeks later, FHA chief Hassell officially withdrew the section from the interstate system. The completion of the north leg of Interstate 240 in 1979 (16 years after the southern leg was finished) helped, as did the realization that the city could keep the astounding sum of $273 million it would have cost to build the road. Still, it took ten more years to undo all the red tape so that the vacant corridor land could be redeveloped as private residences.

The $273 million in interstate substitution funds was doled out for years to other local projects including the downtown trolley. The legacy of the road opponents also endured. A well-organized group of citizens with a good lawyer could change the balance of power. Activists and neighborhood groups have been a force for developers, government, business, and the media to reckon with — or steer clear of — ever since.

In Memoriam: C. H. Butcher Jr.

(The Memphis Flyer, 2002)

C. H. Butcher Jr.

Ever agreeable, C. H. Butcher Jr. posed for this picture in front of the Auction Street Bridge shortly after the trial of U.S. Rep. Harold Ford Sr. in 1993. The bridge was a key part of the government's case against Ford, but Butcher was never called to testify about it. Ironically, at a cost of about $10 million, the bridge has arguably been the most successful economic development stimulus in downtown Memphis because it opened up Mud Island as a residential community of 5,000 people.

In Memoriam: C. H. Butcher Jr.

C. H. Butcher Jr. was the most famous non-witness in the most famous trial in recent Memphis history. Butcher died April 30, 2002, at the age of 63 after a fall in his home near Atlanta. He and his brother Jake, the Democratic candidate for Tennessee governor in 1978, built a Southern banking empire from Knoxville on corruption and fraud. It collapsed in 1982 and 1983, and both brothers did prison time. A notable offshoot of the Butcher banks was the indictment and trial of then-Congressman Harold Ford Sr. of Memphis, who was charged with receiving hundreds of thousands of dollars in loans from the Butchers in exchange for political favors. Ford was acquitted in 1993.

Four years earlier, the government brought Butcher and convicted felon Jesse Barr to Memphis to testify in the first Ford trial, which ended in a mistrial due to juror misconduct. But only Barr was called to the stand to testify. Butcher was too unpredictable or, perhaps, too predictable in his loyalty to Ford and his co-defendants. "He's their friend," said prosecutor Dan Clancy when asked why Butcher didn't testify.

Butcher and Barr spent the days before and during the trial locked up in a jail in rural Arkansas. When I went to interview them for a newspaper story, they were wearing the standard-issue blue chinos and white T-shirts and, I swear, peeling potatoes over the jailhouse stove. I could not detect an ounce of self-pity, depression, or remorse in either of them. Barr was going to testify as an expert on bank fraud, which he had already done many times in rehearsals, debriefings, and even a television interview. When he got done with all this business, he said, he planned to write a book with a raunchy title, which came out as Sex and Southern Politics in my story the next day.

Butcher, amiable and smiling, with hands as big as hams, played straight man to Barr's rogue, feeding him set-up lines and laughing at his jokes. He would have made an interesting witness but wasn't called at the second Ford trial either. Apparently, he was considered too dangerous to the prosecution, which lost the case anyway. After the trial, some of the jurors said they wanted to hear from him.

Butcher was an irrepressible optimist. In the Arkansas jailhouse, he shrugged and said he did not mind hard work one bit because he had done plenty of it as a boy growing up in East Tennessee. He served most of his six years at the federal prison in Atlanta with the hard guys. When inmates rioted and tore up their cells, I was not at all surprised to hear that he had volunteered for cleanup duty in exchange for a reduction of his time.

It pained Butcher that so many people who had grown up like him lost their savings in the collapse of his banks and savings-and-loans, but, of course, it pained the investors even more. Nashville attorney James Neal, who represented Jake Butcher and, briefly, C.H. Butcher, had a simple explanation for Jake's guilty plea. "The facts," he told me, "were so much worse than the indictment."

Twenty years ago, the Butchers and their buddy Bobby Ginn had big plans to develop Mud Island, where they owned an option on a chunk of property. But there was no bridge from downtown, only the causeway at the north end of the island. The publicly funded Auction Street Bridge was designed and approved in 1982 on the mistaken assumption that it would connect to an interstate highway link on Mud Island. Ford was accused of using his influence to get it built as a favor to the Butchers.

The Mud Island property wound up in the hands of the Federal Deposit Insurance Corporation, which sold it to Jack Belz, Henry Turley, and Meredith McCullar for $2.3 million. They developed Harbor Town, which, like every other private development on Mud Island, could not have happened without the Auction Street Bridge.

In a bit of political patronage, the city administration under former Mayor Dick Hackett gave the bridge an honorary name after A.W. Willis Jr., a good man and a civil rights leader who had nothing to do with it. In a different kind of world, it would be named for C.H. Butcher Jr., a good bad man or a bad good man, who had a lot to do with it.

Politics and The Pyramid

(The Commercial Appeal, 1987)

The Pyramid

The Pyramid was supposed to be a Memphis symbol, and in an unintended way that is exactly what it is. Unfortunately, only 13 years after its 1991 grand opening it has come to symbolize failure, political incompetence, and obsolescence now that the FedEx Forum has replaced it. The Pyramid is often maligned even though it served Memphis fairly well, housed the city's first major-league team for three seasons, cost a relatively modest $62 million, and was thoroughly vetted for more than a year. The building's many critics tend to forget all of this.

I was in the chambers of the Memphis City Council and Shelby County Commission when the final votes were taken on funding for The Pyramid and FedEx Forum. Elected officials and board members sharply questioned every aspect, from design to funding to construction schedule. They anticipated many of the problems that came to pass. And yet there was simply no stopping either of them.

History shows that landmark buildings in downtown Memphis got built because someone wealthy, influential, determined, and resourceful wanted them to get built. The Pyramid is supposedly the benchmark for how not to do things, but it seemed like a good idea at the time, and nobody knows how AutoZone Park, Peabody Place, and the FedEx Forum will fare after 13 years.

Politics and The Pyramid

I t was hard to believe last week, watching Mayors Dick Hackett and Bill Morris joking and slapping one another on the back at a joint press conference, that it took so long to come up with a plan for a new arena.

First it was Morris' turn to explain the timing of the decision.

"And there was one more very, very sincere and real reason. If we didn't make a decision on it pretty soon we wouldn't be in office to make a decision.

Several reporters laughed. "At least they're not clapping," joked Hackett.

"My election was last year," quoth Mayor Bill.

"That's another reason this was not made last year," quoth Mayor Dick.

Why did it take so long? Two men who were in on most of the backroom meetings over the past several months — Morris aide Tom Jones and Karl Schledwitz, an attorney who informally represented downtown interests — offer several reasons.

If politicians, like children, find it easier to make up their minds when they don't have so many choices, then Dr. Thomas Carpenter, president of Memphis State University, did the mayors a big favor when he withdrew MSU's support for a downtown arena. "He dealt himself out of the hand," said Jones.

The mayors believed Carpenter was serious a few weeks ago

when he said no MSU money was coming downtown. But after thinking about it a while, they found it hard to believe the Tigers will go it alone. As recently as two months ago, it looked like the arena was going to the Mid-South fairgrounds. Downtown proponents couldn't agree on a site. Jack Belz and Henry Turley wanted it near The Peabody. John Burton Tigrett favored the South Bluff. A. W. Willis Jr. wanted it behind Beale Street. Morris favored the convention center site that eventually was chosen. If downtown backers couldn't come to an agreement, he would support the fairgrounds location, which was easily the most economical. Hackett aide Paul Gurley was a Mid-South Coliseum expansion proponent. Hackett liked the pyramid concept. It proved politically acceptable, with the cost cap at least, and even more so when tied in with the convention center and hotel next door.

"Hackett is wanting to please Morris very much right now," said Schledwitz. He reasons that the only way Hackett can lose the mayor's race is if Morris runs or if Morris and Congressman Harold Ford get behind someone else.

Tigrett feared falling into a trap. If he insisted on the South Bluffs, the mayors might drop the whole idea as they had a year ago. Politics is not his cup of tea. "I'm glad I don't have to make a living in this town," he said during one impasse. He calls the mayors "sport" and "boy."

But downtown and deal-making do interest him at this point in his life, and the pyramid is a big downtown deal. So he carefully specified only a riverside location. Last month Morris and Tigrett took a walking tour of the site. Architect Tony Bologna produced drawings showing how prominently the pyramid stood out when approached from the south on Riverside Drive. Tigrett agreed the north site was acceptable.

Attorney Lewis Donelson served as Tigrett's go-between with the mayors. A site near the convention center was suitable to him. The arena could help the hotel and convention center, although Schledwitz said he did not think hotel and convention center interests were pushing the site.

Last but not least was the glamour factor. The pyramid looked great in pictures.

(Author's note: So it was in 1987. Hackett and Morris would each be

reelected one more time. John Tigrett died in 2002. The site "near the Peabody" became AutoZone Park in 2000. The site "behind Beale Street" became the FedEx Forum and home of the Memphis Grizzlies and the University of Memphis in 2004. The South Bluff is lined with million-dollar homes, and South Bluffs is a popular residential neighborhood. The Mid-South Coliseum is usually empty as is, of course, The Pyramid.)

Suburban City Fathers

(Memphis, 2002)

Cary Whitehead, Jr.

Memphis is big, maybe too big. Play with the numbers and census reports and this is what stands out: 645,000 people living in roughly 300 square miles. Because of a series of annexations after 1950, Memphis tripled its land area and is more than twice the size of Atlanta, St. Louis, Birmingham, or Nashville.

Henry Turley, developer of the HarborTown riverfront planned community and other downtown projects, calls Memphis "the disposable city." An ever-expanding frontier means a constant push for new roads, schools, sewers, and subdivisions, plus a trail of urban blight, half-empty schools, soaring public debt, and abandoned office buildings, hospitals, and sports facilities. Edward Hull Crump, the political boss of Memphis for half a century, would be ashamed at the condition of what he proudly knew as "America's Cleanest City" and "America's Quietest City."

Suburban City Fathers

O
n June 10, 1961, the governor of Mississippi, Ross Barnett, cut a ribbon and officially opened the first subdivision in what would become the city of Southaven. There were balloons, fountains, a man-made lake, and models of cute little $10,000 starter homes on streets named Vaught, Conerly, Gibbs, Poole, and Kinard after Ole Miss football heroes. The cars on Highway 51 backed up for a mile in both directions. The subdivision foretold the thousands of new homes that followed in the next 40 years, swelling the population of Southaven to 29,000 and DeSoto County to 107,000 in Census 2000. And that's as good a starting point as any for the beginning of suburban Memphis.

The developer of Southaven was a 35-year-old Memphian and Ole Miss graduate named Cary Whitehead, Jr. He was gregarious and movie-star handsome in a Kennedyesque way and, fittingly, had been getting white-headed since before his 30th birthday. His partners were the better-known home builder/ Holiday Inns team of Kemmons Wilson and Wallace Johnson. Each of them owned 30 percent of the company and Whitehead owned 40 percent. A few weeks before the grand opening, Johnson telephoned Whitehead to tell him the newspaper wanted to take some pictures and interview the founders. There was just one thing. How exactly, Johnson asked, do you get to Southaven? Well, Whitehead said, you take Lamar to Bellevue, which is Highway 51, and you turn left and keep going until you see the damnedest subdivision you ever saw. Johnson found it all right, and when he got in front of the camera and started waving his arms around and talking about how "me 'n' Kimmons seen this" and "me 'n' Kimmons seen that," it gave Whitehead a story he still cackles over 40 years later.

Because he, not Johnson or Wilson, was the detail man, the mathematician, the land scout with an almost photographic memory for real estate who bought 2,600 acres in DeSoto County in 1959. He was the one who told Ross Barnett that if someone built a suburb up there the blacks, who were mostly poor and living in shacks with outhouses, would leave and the whites would come. Whitehead understood white flight and the lure of low taxes, he understood politics, and he knew Memphis was on an annexation kick, taking in Frayser in 1958 and eyeing Raleigh and Whitehaven. Thousands of the future residents of DeSoto County would come from the other side of the Tennessee state line in Whitehaven — so many that Whitehead almost named the new town South Whitehaven until deciding to lop off a syllable.

The keys to making it work, then as now, were sewers and schools. Mississippi Power & Light was glad to have the new customers and put in the power. The county built a new elementary school that was projected to have 700 students but had 900 by 1963. And Whitehead, Johnson, and Wilson formed Allied Investment Company, which built the sewage treatment plant.

So rapid was the growth that Whitehead would thenceforth believe that the single greatest truth of the development business was this: He who controls the sanitary sewer rules the world.

Whitehaven in the Sixties was, among other things, exactly that: a haven for whites. Its nexus was the intersection of Shelby Drive and Highway 51, site of the Southland Mall, which opened in 1966. Its residents included Elvis Presley, a future mayor of Memphis named Dick Hackett, and one Waymon "Jackie" Welch Jr., whose father was in the real estate business. Thanks in no small part to Southaven, the real estate business in Whitehaven was about to become a very interesting business to be in. When the new mall came in, the city and county rezoned Highway 51, now known as Elvis Presley Boulevard, from residential to commercial.

Whitehaven was a close-knit community where a lot of the older residents knew Waymon Welch Sr., who was head of the Homebuilders Association. When their property was rezoned, they asked him to sell it. Young Jackie Welch was no great shakes in school, but he got by when he had to, and he learned most of his lessons on the streets anyway. Once a noted Golden Gloves boxer came up to him at a pool hall and bet him $25 he could whip him, and Welch went out in the parking lot and beat him up, then grabbed him by the neck and demanded his $25. Welch compiled a list of the properties along Highway 51 and Shelby Drive and started to market them to gas stations, restaurants, banks, and the increasingly popular fast-food places. In doing that he kick-started his career in the commercial real estate business, where he would later cross paths with Cary Whitehead.

The highs and lows of their careers over the next 30 years would shape the growth of suburban Memphis and Shelby County including Southaven, Hickory Hill, Cordova, Shelby Farms, and the extension of the all-important Grey's Creek Sewer east of Cordova.

The next time Cary Whitehead left a lasting mark on Memphis real estate it was not for something he built but for something he helped stop from being built: a huge planned community at Shelby Farms.

Shelby Farms sits squarely in the center of the city's prime growth corridor, bounded today on the west by Baptist Hospital East and on the east by Germantown Parkway and the Cordova subdivisions. At 4,500 acres, it is the largest urban park in the country, more than five times the size of New York's Central Park. In fact it is bigger than the Gettysburg or Shiloh military parks.

No one planned it that way, as demonstrated by the hodgepodge of current uses including a prison, park, lakes, wilderness trails, pasture, third-rate soccer fields, a restaurant, Ducks Unlimited's headquarters, Agricenter International, and experimental agriculture. Throughout the 1960s and early 1970s, with growth lapping at the western edges of the park, there was strong sentiment to develop some of it. A coalition of First National Bank (now First Tennessee), Boyle Investment Company, and the nationally prominent planning firm The Rouse Corporation wanted to buy approximately half of the park and build a planned community.

Rouse was willing to let local developers do the single-family housing. It would do the more-profitable commercial and multi-family housing on the high ground north of Walnut Grove Road. Rouse would "assist" the city and county in developing parks, golf courses, a zoo, or whatever it wanted on the rest of the land — all of which, of course, would enhance its own development. The proposed 8,000 housing units would dry up development in East Memphis for years. The plan was endorsed by a study done by a firm called American Cities, which, it turned out, was wholly owned by Rouse.

A coalition of environmentalists and developers formed against the Rouse plan, or "the Shelby Farms land grab" as it came to be known on a bumper sticker. Whitehead and his attorney, John Porter of Burch Porter and Johnson, were at the forefront.

Nothing if not combative, Whitehead was a formidable figure. He had stage presence, command of details, and a wicked tongue when he needed it. He had nothing against development of Shelby Farms per se. He was a developer, after all, and knew better than anyone that the land Rouse proposed to buy was probably worth almost $50 million at the time. He had far more in common with Boyle, where he had once worked and where his son is now senior vice president, than with the young, idealistic, long-haired environmentalists. Yet he became their ally. He could debate the proponents on their terms, or turn his sarcasm on a planner's "Veronica Lake" haircut. At one particularly noisy and well-publicized public meeting, he and Porter dramatically exposed the Rouse-American Cities connection, and Porter thundered that "this fraud shall not stand."

Momentum shifted in the opponents' favor, and when the recession hit in 1974, the deal was dead and Rouse withdrew. At about the same time, environmentalists and their lawyers were stopping a proposed extension of Interstate 40 through Overton Park. There would be other proposals to systematically develop Shelby Farms over the next 30 years, but none of them has gotten anywhere. Opposition to the Rouse plan became opposition to any development at all. Shelby Farms, like Overton Park which is one-twelfth its size, is sacred ground. That is why suburban sprawl leapfrogs the park and resumes four miles to the east. Its Main Street is Germantown Parkway. Its Southaven is Cordova. Its land of opportunity is the Grey's Creek Basin.

Whitehead's career faltered in the years after the Shelby Farms debate. Even if Shelby Farms was off limits, a restless Memphis was not going to sit still. Development simply moved to other areas of the city or county where opposition wasn't so formidable. By the mid-1970s, the spirit of Watergate had shined its light on all sorts of public corruption. Memphis land deals, zoning, and roadbuilding drew the attention of the FBI and the United States Attorney's Office. Whitehead and a County Squire named Lee Hyden were among those caught in the net. Whitehead pleaded guilty to loan fraud. In a separate, highly publicized case that helped speed the transformation of the old County Court into the Shelby County Commission, he testified for prosecutor Hickman Ewing Jr. that Hyden had demanded kickbacks from him in exchange for running roads through Whitehead's property. Hyden did three-and-a-half years in prison, after which he got religion and became a minister. Whitehead did 86 days at the federal minimum-security prison at Eglin Air Force Base, after which he resumed his career as a developer.

He was a walking encyclopedia of local real estate, and in 1990 the Homebuilders Association made him chairman of its developers' council and liaison with the City Council. He liked to call himself the Old Indian Fighter because he could read the signs so well — the stakes with little red flags tied to them that meant road widening was coming; the subtle changes in zoning or deviations from the major road plan that meant someone's property had just gotten a lot more valuable; the warranty deeds in the *Daily News* that recorded ownership changes; the aerial maps that showed water and topography, because topography determines drainage and development costs and density; and the way land looked in the spring when it was raining. But he was not the force he had once been.

The force he had once been was named Jackie Welch. After he cut his teeth on Whitehaven commercial real estate, Welch moved his young family to a subdivision off of Germantown Road and turned his attention to southeast Shelby County, where the Whitehaven process was being repeated on a more spacious scale. The nexus was Ridgeway and Winchester and the Hickory Ridge Mall. Welch started buying small lots and tracts of land up and down Winchester. Welch Realty sold, by his estimation, half of the land along Winchester, dealing

with many of the same oil companies, restaurants, car dealers, and
retailers he had dealt with in Whitehaven.

To Welch, real estate wasn't that different from the car business
or the clothing business. You had to know your product and not get
outside your expertise, not venture into industrial development or
something you knew nothing about. You made sure you knew the old
families who own the large tracts of land, or you took on partners who
did. You worked with builders who didn't put up junk. You networked
with the politicians and were generous with the fund-raisers and
contributions. You needed the cunning of a master turkey hunter,
Welch's favorite hobby. And you dealt with land every day, day after
day, for years.

Welch liked to say that he might not be the hardest worker or the
smartest guy in the world, but he knew one thing beyond question,
and that was the value of a piece of land.

Whitehead and Welch don't like each other. That is not exactly
right. When you put two bulls in the same pasture, they are bound to
fight. They were partners, sort of, for a little while in the Winchester
area in the 1980s, and engineer Jim Dickinson, who is now Welch's
partner, did some work for Whitehead Properties on a project called
the Villages of Bennington. Welch, like Whitehead, has also been
partners in some deals with Kemmons Wilson. Welch said he admires
Whitehead's brains and accomplishments. Whitehead simply said
they drew a line in the sand and leaves it at that. Neither man wants
to go into it.

In southeast Shelby County Welch was working mostly outside
the Memphis city limits, where he had a very good friend and a new
customer who would put him ahead of the pack. The friend was Jim
Rout, and the new customer was the Shelby County Board of Education.

Rout, who attended Sherwood Elementary School with Welch,
was on the Shelby County Commission from 1979 to 1994, when he
became county mayor. Rout introduced Welch to Jim Anderson, the
superintendent of the county schools. Anderson explained the county's
selection criteria for new school sites in terms of major roads, parking,
frontage, and acreage. Welch Realty was already one of the primary
developers and brokers in the area, and it soon became the school
board's favorite real estate vendor. Welch sold the sites for Kirby High

School, Kirby Middle School, and Southwind Elementary School. Then he went up Germantown Parkway and did the same thing in Cordova and Berryhill.

In approximately 15 years Welch Realty sold nine school sites. The county school board bought other sites from other brokers, but of all the sites Welch showed, he never showed them one they did not buy. "The only problem was the secret got out," he said with a slight smile. "I kind of had the franchise for a while."

Even if Welch didn't make a profit on the school site, and usually he did, he made it on the subdivisions he developed around the schools because the schools were magnets for growth. Schools and subdivisions required new roads, and roads meant corners, and commercial corners were the icing on the cake, the biggest, sweetest caramel in the whole box. Welch got $150,000 for a bank site, or a gas station, or a restaurant. For two acres at the corner of Berryhill and Chimneyrock he got $600,000 from Walgreens, and he said he had virtually "nothing" in the lot. The rooftops and schools made it possible, but you've got to sell several $40,000 lots to make $600,000. Welch Realty has sold and developed 3,971 lots. Little wonder he said that "every time I sold a school site, I called and thanked Commissioner Rout for having the foresight."

The toughest nut to crack was Cordova High School. If Welch had anything to say about it, it would be named Jim Rout High School. Because in his eyes, Rout brought the city sewer to the Grey's Creek Basin and unclogged the biggest pipeline of them all. In 1969 the city of Memphis took over responsibility for extending the sewer from the county, which got The Med and Juvenile Court in the bargain. Some 20 years later, developers began to apply pressure on the city to extend the sewer to the wedge of land called the Grey's Creek Basin east of Cordova. Mayor Dick Hackett wouldn't go for it, and the City Council wouldn't go for it, and for years Mayor Willie Herenton wouldn't go for it. Any extension of the sewer would spur growth outside the city. The sewer would cost $20 million to build, and it would open not just a few subbasins but the entire basin. Roads, utilities, and fire and police services, city officials warned, would be expensive if the entire basin was opened and scattered development occurred. In theory, Memphis could annex the areas, but in fact annexations often took several years and sparked a backlash of resentment.

By 1997 the county was clamoring for new schools to serve all the subdivisions that had been put in between Germantown and Bartlett. Rout promised the county schools they would have a sewer in the Grey's Creek Basin even if the county had to build a sewage lagoon itself. He instructed Anderson to get two school sites — one for Cordova High School and the other for a new elementary school nearby.

Anderson turned to Welch. Welch and Dickinson had assembled 400 acres for a good price because it was a mile outside the sewered area. Sewer would double the value of the land. Welch sold 45 acres to the county schools for his cost of $17,600 an acre, or $792,000 total. Rout cut the deal with the city to build the sewer. The city council and Mayor Herenton relented in exchange for an annexation agreement, a "balanced growth" plan for future development, and a plan to allow the city and county to share the new high school.

The schools got the sewer, and so did Welch, who was able to develop 1,500 more lots and tie them into the new sewer for an additional fee of $1,000 per lot. With the subsequent extension of the sewer to Highway 64, the entire Grey's Creek Basin was opened for development.

Census 2000 shows that the Memphis and Shelby County portions of Cordova and surrounding areas have a population of 57,686 — a 93 percent increase over 1990. The Cordova area is larger than Bartlett, Germantown, or Collierville. Cordova High School has an enrollment of 2,100 students and will graduate its first class of seniors this year. Projections are that the Grey's Creek Basin area will grow by another 48,000 residents in the next 20 years.

He who controls the sanitary sewer rules the world.

Jackie Welch and Donna, his wife of 36 years, live in an astonishing new 7,000-foot home in Collierville. It has two man-made ponds, stocked with bass, bream, and Japanese koi. Their daughters live in new homes next door, although next door is a lot farther away than it was in Whitehaven or Hickory Hill. Welch's latest project is Devonshire Gardens, a subdivision to surpass all subdivisions, on a choice piece of property north of Poplar Avenue in Germantown. The planned community includes 129 lots that sell for $145,000 to $200,000 apiece. When finished it will consist entirely of million-dollar homes.

Except a funny thing happened. Developers overdid the high-end housing market in Collierville, Germantown, Southwind, even rural Eads. Sales were slow in 2000, and that was before the stock market crash. It was as if the gods of sprawl looked at all the tract mansions with bathrooms with saunas and Jacuzzis and closets big enough to park a truck and said, "Enough of this conceit! Let's see how you like Nasdaq 1600!" By March, Welch had sold nine lots. "All I need," he joked, "is 120 more millionaires."

He may not get them this year or the next. Maybe he even overstepped himself for a change. But he's come a hell of a long way from Whitehaven, you gotta give him that.

Hit and Miss

(Memphis, 2000)

AutoZone Park

AutoZone Park is the home of the Memphis Redbirds, the AAA affiliate of the St. Louis Cardinals. It is the most expensive minor-league baseball stadium in the country and, so far at least, one of the leaders in annual attendance. The Grammy Museum never came to be, but it was a sign of how badly Memphis wanted to play in the big leagues. It was a bump in the road. A year later, the NBA and the Grizzlies would come to town. It was no mere coincidence that during this time span, two able public officials at the center of events — Center City Commission Executive Director Ed Armentrout and county mayoral aide Tom Jones — lost their jobs for misuse of expense accounts and county credit cards. Memphis was in the big time, and big money was part of it.

Hit and Miss

Sometime on the afternoon of April 1st, St. Louis Cardinals slugger Mark McGwire will step to the plate at AutoZone Park, wiggle his bat a few times, and if there is any good baseball karma in Memphis, hit a monstrous home run that will arch into the sky and land somewhere in the vicinity of Danny Thomas Boulevard.

The cheers of 15,000 fans at the exhibition game will punctuate the opening of what Memphis hopes will be its own home run — the finest and most expensive minor-league baseball stadium in the country. At $72 million, AutoZone Park is the centerpiece of a redeveloped section of downtown that also includes the $30 million Toyota Center, an $8 million parking garage, a $36 million apartment building, and a $15 million public school. Few people thought minor-league baseball, doomed by definition to meaningless games and sudden call-ups of its best players, had such power to change the face of Memphis. On a good night at Tim McCarver Stadium, a few thousand people would be in the stands to watch the Memphis Chicks. Apathy was one of the reasons the team moved to a new home in Jackson, Tennessee, after the 1997 season.

That was about when sports reporter George Lapides phoned his old friend Dean Jernigan with an urgent appeal, the gist of which was, "You can't let them take our team." In jock-speak, Jernigan stepped up. His grand slam brought in an expansion AAA franchise, the Cardinals affiliation, a new stadium, and $89 million of additional development. Now his bigger-than-baseball vision, the nonprofit foundation that owns the team, and the sponsor-laden financing package that is building the stadium are the model for other developments like the riverfront promenade.

"Who else was going to do it?" asks Jernigan, the founder and chief executive of Storage USA. "I felt an obligation. I had learned a good bit about baseball with Avron Fogelman when he owned the Chicks, and the Chicks were leaving."

Granted, the Redbirds are on a honeymoon, but Jernigan connected with his hometown in a way few people have, with pitches rarely seen. The Pyramid, Mud Island, the Grammy Museum, the Tennessee Oilers, and the Convention Center have sputtered or died for lack of support. Why then is AutoZone Park flush with sponsors and goodwill? Part of the answer, oddly enough, is the failure of other sports ventures in Memphis. Nashville has the NFL Titans and the NHL Predators, and both play in new publicly financed facilities and compete for corporate marketing dollars. In Memphis, which is roughly the same size as Nashville, the Redbirds are the only pro game in town now that the RiverKings hockey team is headed for Mississippi. "We wouldn't strap on two of these," said Kent Richey, owner of Covington Pike Toyota, one of three Memphis dealers involved in a $1.25 million Redbirds sponsorship that gives it naming rights to an office building and parking garage.

But Toyota and other companies were willing and able to strap on one. Toyota and AutoZone both bid for the naming rights to the stadium before AutoZone won the deal for $4.5 million over 15 years. Coca-Cola will pay another $3.75 million for pouring rights for 15 years. Bryan Foods, Powertel, and Baptist Hospital all signed six-figure deals for five years. The 48 club suites sold out at $38,000 to $45,000 a year for 15 years — a stiff price but a bargain relative to the NFL or the NHL. Putting your name on one of the 217 bronze baseballs in The Plaza costs $2,500. Seat plaques go for $50 to $500.

Despite small crowds in Memphis, minor-league baseball is hot, especially when played in a nostalgic ballpark modeled after Camden Yards in Baltimore or Jacobs Field in Cleveland. Louisville, Indianapolis, and Oklahoma City have recently built neotraditional stadiums near their downtowns. In all, 90 cities have built new minor-league baseball stadiums since 1985, most of them after 1990 when the National Association of Professional Baseball Leagues set new standards for ballparks. Total attendance for the 172 minor-league clubs topped 35 million in 1998, almost double the attendance 10 years ago. Those trends helped, but Jernigan had more important things going for him. His wife Kristi is a full partner, defining a new role for women in Memphis and, in her own way, as influential a downtown player as any woman since Pat Tigrett. Dean Jernigan has Memphis connections going all the way back to Messick High School, where he graduated a few years after Shelby County Mayor Jim Rout. He played hardball with reluctant bankers and took the IRS to extra innings over the tax-exempt status (later revoked) of the bonds financing stadium construction. And he invested $20,000 in a picture that turned out to be worth a thousand words and $72 million.

"Window dressing?" Kristi Jernigan laughed. "Sometimes I wish I was. What people don't realize is that maybe we've made this look too easy. Dean's running a New York Stock Exchange company full time and is a very active CEO. If we were going to do this, I had to get involved."

A native of Savannah, Tennessee, and a CPA by trade, she is a self-described "good casual fan."

"I always say I have to have something else to keep me interested the whole game," she said. "I think I contributed to the design of the ballpark as someone who wasn't just there to watch the game. My and Dean's influence is everywhere. I remember being in a meeting about the roof where one of the architects said, 'Well, half of my client wants the roof turned up and the other half of my client wants the roof turned down.' So we have this roof that turns up on the end, dips down, then turns up again like a hat over the press box."

A big part of her job early on was working with the Washington, D.C., law firm that drew up the nonprofit application for the foundation that owns the team. It is the only such arrangement in professional baseball. "Dean has been through the professional sports scene and kind of exited it with a bad taste in his mouth. We didn't want to be in the newspapers every day with someone asking if we're lining our pockets off a community asset." The nonprofit application took six months, but it earned the Redbirds and the Jernigans instant credibility and defused public cynicism during the two years when baseball in Memphis was basically running on fumes.

After he returned to Memphis from Baltimore in 1992, Jernigan had not planned to get involved with baseball again. He played short-stop at Messick, losing to Steve Spurrier's Johnson City team in the state playoffs one year. After college he joined the Army, where he was a helicopter pilot. After a short stint as a Memphis sportswriter, he went to work for brothers Robert and Avron Fogelman in their apartment business. Avron Fogelman owned the Memphis Chicks and, later, half of the Kansas City Royals, so Jernigan had an inside knowledge of the game and the egos involved in it. He was head of the Memphis Sports Authority in 1984 but had none of Fogelman's flair for publicity. Jernigan split with Fogelman that year, two years before the Fogelman real estate limited partnerships crashed. With venture capital from Memphis commodities trader Willard Sparks, he started Storage USA, a national chain of self-storage facilities. Not incidentally, he moved to Baltimore in 1988 where he became a fan of the Orioles and their new stadium, Camden Yards, which is in many ways the model for AutoZone Park. Storage USA went public in 1994, and Jernigan owns about $20 million worth of stock. That gave him the financial cushion to get reinvolved with baseball and apply his own take-charge methods.

His first thought was to buy the Memphis Chicks from owner David Hersh, who had been badgering the city, county, and Memphis fans for more support for years. He called Rick Masson, the chief administrative officer for the city of Memphis, and asked if he would meet with him and Jim Rout, who were both in New York at the time. Sure, said Masson, whenever you get back. No, Jernigan said, the meeting had to be right away. Masson and City of Memphis Finance Director Roland McElrath flew to New York that day to discuss form-ing a public-private partnership to buy the Chicks. Rout was already on board. At the county building, the joke is that anyone from Messick High School, where both the mayor and his wife Sandy grad-uated, goes right in the door. With no appetite for chasing Hersh, Jernigan hatched another plan.

"I like having alternatives, and I wondered if it was possible to get another franchise for Memphis," said Jernigan. "I knew the chair-man of the AAA expansion committee, and he said they would like nothing better than to get an application from Memphis. We put in our application, and I told Hersh we were withdrawing our offer and he could take his team to Jackson."

Jernigan began laying the groundwork for the new stadium even before he had a team. He shunned the standard practice of doing feasibility studies and hiring consultants. "It never even occurred to me," he said. Going against his instincts which told him the stadium should be out east, he turned his back on a suburban site in the heart of baseball's white fan base, and started driving around downtown with Kristi and visions of a smaller version of Camden Yards. Early on, he envisioned a project that would be more than a ballpark, with a public park and office buildings incorporated into the design. He knew he could move the headquarters of Storage USA into some of the space, and he got a commitment from his architects, Looney Ricks Kiss Architects, as well. But first he had to get some land without alerting every speculator in downtown.

"He put $135,000 in Interstate Realty Company as escrow money, set the range of prices we would pay, said 'OK, do it,' and that was the last direction I got," said Earl Blankenship, who secretly assembled the 12 mostly blighted acres of downtown that included a porno theater and two large empty buildings. "He absolutely will not tolerate procrastination."

Twenty of the 40 parcels were under contract before the announcement of the baseball site was made and before Jernigan even had a guarantee that Memphis would get one of the two expansion AAA franchises available. The $8.5 million used to buy the land and a state sales tax rebate are the only public appropriations. With a dream, a hole in the ground, and the singular combination of patience and zeal required to sit through 70 minor-league baseball games a year, the sales team set about raising the rest from sponsors. Kristi Jernigan gives some of the credit for the early sales successes to a $20,000 color rendering produced by a computer-assisted design firm.

"Twenty thousand dollars seemed like an incredible amount of money at that time, but when you think of how much inventory we sold off of that picture it was more than worth it because it made people see The Peabody and the street and the skyline," she said. "In this case a picture was really worth a thousand words."

At $72 million, AutoZone Park is no ordinary minor-league ball-park. Louisville, Oklahoma City, and Indianapolis each spent around $20-$35 million on their AAA stadiums. The Jernigans shrug off the difference. Memphis is in a seismic zone. Publicly funded stadiums lowball their costs. The $72 million includes $8.5 million for land assembly, and although there are no gold door knobs at AutoZone Park, they admit they went first class.

"When the architects asked for the budget, I told them to show us the best design," said Dean. "Memphis is notorious for not building the best we could, for always cutting corners. Kristi and I pledged that we would not do that. People are going to see that we really did do something right."

Baseball wasn't supposed to be center stage in Memphis this year. This is the year the National Academy of Recording Arts and Sciences (NARAS) was supposed to tell the world about the long-awaited opening of the Grammy Expo and Hall of Fame in Memphis.

But last year, after more than two years of coast-to-coast schmoozing and $800,000, Memphis Grammy boosters gave up the ghost on a deal that once promised to link two of the most recognizable names in music in the world. If there is a lesson in there, it is this: in Memphis, individuals are the driving force behind successful projects. Projects by committee don't happen, no matter how attractive the idea may seem at a glance.

If AutoZone Park set a standard for doing more with less, Memphis' 25-year courtship of the Grammy music museum surely holds the record for doing less with more. Take 600,000 Elvis fans and The Pyramid and you have . . . Graceland and a big empty space. On the other hand, maybe the Grammy-Memphis marriage was never meant to be. The first Grammy awards were handed out in 1958. Henry Mancini, Perry Como, Ella Fitzgerald, and Domenico Modugno (he sang "Volare" but not the one you remember by Bobby Rydell) took the top honors. The same year, Jerry Lee Lewis sold 12 million copies of "Whole Lotta Shakin' Going On," "Great Balls of Fire," and "Breathless." Elvis Presley went in the Army, but RCA Records released "I Got Stung," "Hard Headed Woman," "One Night," and "Wear My Ring Around Your Neck."

Nice work, guys, but no Grammy for you. The King would later win three Grammies, all in the gospel category, putting him two ahead of the noted songstress Hillary Rodham Clinton, who won a Grammy a few years ago. The Killer, however, was a dead man at Grammy time, unless you count a 1986 award in the "spoken word" category — the same category in which Hillary was honored, making it one of the most unlikely pairings in music history.

It seems like only yesterday that the Memphis Area Chamber of Commerce announced that Memphis was competing with New York, Atlanta, Nashville, and Los Angeles for the NARAS Hall of Fame. Actually, it was 1975. By 1982, the selection process was "down to the wire," according to NARAS, with Memphis and Atlanta ready for "final inspection." The Hall of Fame, backed by $8 million in bonds issued by the Center City Revenue Finance Corporation, was supposed to bring in 550,000 visitors a year. Nothing happened. NARAS and Memphis went their separate ways. Later that year, Graceland opened to the public and did in fact attract over 500,000 visitors. Beale Street also reopened. There were problems galore, but at least Memphis was back on the music map.

The televised Grammy awards ceremony became an international hit, with a broader focus than the nostalgia-oriented Rock and Roll Hall of Fame in Cleveland (which has no connection with NARAS). Memphians and former Memphians get their share of attention from time to time, although with 98 categories and five nominees per category, so does just about everyone else. Al Green and B.B. King have collected 17 Grammy awards between them. A Memphis NARAS chapter carries the torch for local music.

The Memphis-Grammy affair refused to die, partly because NARAS was unable to make a deal with Chicago, New Orleans, Los Angeles, Atlanta, Toronto, or anyone else for a museum/exposition and hall of fame. In 1994, NARAS President Michael Greene came to Memphis and visited Beale Street, which by then had been revived by the opening of B.B. King's club. There was talk of possibly doing something there, but it never amounted to anything.

"Michael Greene isn't really pushing this, but he's a Southerner and he has a soft spot for Memphis," said Richard Ranta, dean of the College of Communication and Fine Arts at the University of Memphis, and a NARAS member and friend of Greene for nearly 20 years. "He wants the best deal for NARAS, a nonprofit that lives off a single source of television revenue. He's not in a position to put up $10 million. His job is to market their good name."

The bait to lure NARAS was The Pyramid. The city and county put out requests for proposals to fill the empty space at the top and bottom. Both NARAS and Dick Clark's American Music Hall of Fame showed interest, although neither had financing. The governments tentatively agreed to go instead with Memphian Marius Penczner's proposal for a high-tech interactive attraction, "Island Earth EcoCenter," pitched as a something-besides-music alternative.

At the eleventh hour, the agreement was scrapped by the city, much to the surprise of county Mayor Jim Rout. Songwriter David Porter, author of "Soul Man" and other hits, and developer Henry Turley persuaded Mayor Willie Herenton to reconsider a music attraction instead. "You may not have killed it (Island Earth)," Rout told Turley, "but your fingerprints are all over the murder weapon."

Turley didn't deny it. He scoffed at Penczner's idea as a glorified video arcade with no connection to the one thing for which Memphis was known around the world, namely its music. And the Grammy courtship began again, in earnest. The game plan featured an impressive ensemble cast of downtown players: Turley, the Center City Commission, John Stokes of Morgan Keegan, Tom Garrott of National Bank of Commerce, businessman Scott Ledbetter, architect Greg Hnedak, and Blues Ball organizer Pat Tigrett. John Tigrett, the father of The Pyramid, was a backstage supporter, later added to the NARAS board. The local NARAS chapter would try to raise $1 million by selling 65,000 memberships.

"Grammy is a huge and transforming deal, and we can't let anything stand in the way of our realizing its full potential," Turley wrote to Blankenship and Ledbetter in January 1997. "There's consensus in the Memphis business community that getting the Grammy Hall of Fame is a top priority for the city. Both mayors are aboard and it seems we have a financing mechanism put together to raise the requisite money."

All of those assumptions would prove to be wrong or shaky, but for two years the Grammy backers gave it their best shot. They met in Memphis. They met in Los Angeles. They met in Las Vegas, where they saw a "high-tech show with 250 special effects" by Seventies teen idol David Cassidy of Partridge Family fame. They twice went to the Grammy show at Madison Square Garden, doling out $850 tickets to Memphians deemed to be influential enough to matter in the rarefied world of NARAS.

The majority of the $800,000 spent to lure NARAS went to consultants. Design consultant Landmark Entertainment, favored by Greene, signed up for $300,000. Hnedak was hired to do the local cost controls. Consultant Dana Nottingham would "provide strategic planning and development management during the concept design phase" for $190,000. There was sponsorship consultant Edward Dorris, who — prophetically as it turned out — noted the "dismal results" for the sponsorship and donor efforts for the Rock and Roll Hall of Fame and Museum in Cleveland. Feasibility consultant, the Lyon Group, said the "GEAR" (Grammy Expo and a restaurant) would have annual operating revenue of $17 million and profits of $5 million. The list went on and on until "we had consultants watching consultants," according to Tom Jones, chief aide to Mayor Rout.

One thing they did not have was a clear picture of exactly what it was they were after. Landmark Entertainment had a video it had peddled in other cities. Ledbetter admits he and others were dazzled, although it later dawned on them that they could have a similar experience in a lounge chair with a beer in their hands, watching television. Greene insisted it be called an exposition instead of a museum because of the boring guitars-under-glass connotations of a music museum. The central exhibit would be a "music tree" leading to different interactive exhibits on all kinds of American music from classical to Broadway. "They wanted to serve us guacamole and we wanted barbecue," said lawyer James McLaren, who negotiated with Greene and Landmark for the Center City Commission.

Museum or expo, the details were fuzzy, and government enthusiasm was underwhelming. After looking at one of the early designs, Jones pointed out that less than 10 percent of the space would go to Memphis music, about the same as the classical music component. The cost, initially pegged at around $50 million, soared to nearly $100 million. The debt service on that would far exceed operating revenues under even the best scenarios. Ledbetter, who was closely involved with the expansion of the Memphis Zoo and the Memphis Museum System, knew that most tourist attractions are lucky to break even. The Pyramid has a distinctive design, a nice view 300 feet above the Mississippi River, and 20,000 seats. The arena takes up only half the space, leaving 250,000 feet to develop. But the only connection between the bottom and the top is an interior staircase. And there is no true front door because of the railroad tracks. Hnedak estimated that a Front Street grand entrance and transit terminal would add $15 to 20 million to the cost.

Nobody was willing to put up that kind of money, or any money at all beyond the expenses of the inclinator to the top, which would come out of public funds, and the cost of consultants and entertainment, which was picked up by the Center City Commission or the Downtown Leadership Council. Publicly, Memphis' Grammy backers put up a brave front, celebrating a "contract" between the Center City Development Commission and NARAS, and predicting a grand opening sometime in late 1999. Despite a lack of tangible progress, a delegation again flew to New York for the 1998 Grammy awards show, throwing a big party for Greene at the exclusive restaurant Club 21 for $12,477.

Behind the wining and dining and the upbeat facade, the house of cards was collapsing in bickering and mistrust. The consultants were squabbling with each other and with the Center City Commission, and the NARAS relationship was disintegrating. "NARAS has been little help in identifying prospective sponsors and has resisted approaching their existing sponsors," the Center City Commission complained. "NARAS has done virtually nothing on helping us get intellectual property for the attraction. Without images and music, we don't have much."

There was no single driving force, no man with a plan. Greene had a strong voice in decision making, but the city and county were being asked to put the money up to develop the concept. The Los Angeles Times published a series of articles questioning Greene's stewardship of the nonprofit NARAS Foundation, which gave him a $700,000 bonus in 1997. In New York, an aide to Mayor Rudolph Giuliani argued with Greene over the mayor's role in announcing Grammy nominees, leading Giuliani to suggest that the awards ceremony could return to Los Angeles for all he cared.

For several months, the talks continued between the Center City Commission and NARAS, but the fire was out. It was a mopping-up operation, a long goodbye to justify all the time and money that had been spent as much as anything.

"I don't view it as something Memphis lost," said Rout. "Memphis never really had it." Or maybe had "it" all along, and Beale Street, Graceland, the Smithsonian Rock 'n' Soul Exhibition, Horseshoe Casino's Bluesville, the Stax Museum of American Soul Music, and the elusive Grammy museum are just attempts to catch it in a bottle and put a fancy wrapper around it. Jeff Sanford, executive director of the Center City Commission, recalls a dinner he had with John Tigrett shortly before he died last year. The conversation came around to NARAS and the problems with the Grammy deal.

"You need a crazy man," Tigrett said.

The more he thought about it, Sanford came to believe that Tigrett was exactly right.

VI.
Tough Guys

Dago: The Toughest
Man in Memphis

(Mid-South magazine, 1985; The Memphis Flyer, 2004)

Charles Tiller (Dago)

What little I know about the science of penology I learned while following Charles Tiller from prison to prison across the state of Tennessee. Stonney Lane, the former warden at Brushy Mountain Prison in Petros where Tiller and James Earl Ray were incarcerated for several years, told me Tiller was an inmate to be reckoned with by both guards and fellow inmates because of his uncommon intelligence and strength. Tiller was a good student and star athlete in Memphis in the Fifties before he became a brawler and a killer. He died in 2004, never recovering from being beaten with a baseball bat by fellow inmates ten years earlier at the state penitentiary in Nashville. It wasn't until after his funeral that I learned the origin of his nickname. A coach once said "he runs like a little Dago" and the name stuck.

Dago: The Toughest
Man in Memphis

"You are about to sail out from the sheltered, secure, carefree harbor of home and youth, into the seething, surging, confusing, dangerous seas of adult life... There will be storms as well as happy, peaceful days in your life's course; cross winds must needs disturb your planned course. There will be heart-breaking disappointments, soul searing crosses. Mary, sinless, the mother of God, was yet the mother of sorrows."

> – William L. Adrian, Bishop of Nashville, in a letter to
> the 1954 graduating class of Christian Brothers High
> School in Memphis.

Dago.

Now it seems like a strange nickname for a non-Italian who grew up and went to school with boys with names like Torti and Grisanti and Pierotti. But these were the 1950s, before ethnic consciousness became a national issue, and the name was not a slur but a mark of friendship like Spike or Butch or Red. It is still the name many of his classmates use when they talk about their old friend Charles Tiller.

A little luck and a little more ability and he might have been another one of those great big league infielders from the South, tough, fearless and mean like Eddie Stanky. Or if there had been a war going on he would have made a great soldier.

Or he might have been a doctor, dentist, or lawyer, like many of his friends at Christian Brothers High School, class of 1954. He was

popular, nice-looking, smart and athletic. By the end of his third year
in college he was already accepted to medical school.

But it didn't work out that way. Charles Tiller made a name for
himself all right but not for his athletic talents. His buddies got the
jobs as lawyers, policemen, surgeons and businessmen here in
Memphis. Charles Tiller is in the state prison at Fort Pillow serving
two 100-year sentences on a double-murder conviction.

Anyone who lived around Memphis in the 1960s and 1970s and
read the newspapers had heard of Dago Tiller and his cousins and
their reputation as tough guys. They were in the news on and off
for 20 years for a long series of arrests, mostly for fighting. It got so
the reporters started keeping a sort of box score of their arrests, and in
the later years, if one were arrested the others were likely to be mentioned too, just to fill out the history. Not that there weren't some wild
stories about barroom brawls, fights with the police, a couple of sexual
assaults. The Tiller Boys Tear Up Memphis. It was better than The
Untouchables.

But before all that, Charles Tiller was in another part of the
paper and had a different reputation as one of the best all-around high
school athletes in the city. He played baseball in the summer American
Legion League, which was big time then, with the games and scores
written up in the newspaper and the talent drawn from all over the
city. Corbitt Motors' team went 14-1 in 1953, winning the state
championship and finishing second in the Southeast region. Tiller
played second base and batted leadoff and made all-city, all-state, and
all-Southeast. On one team he edged out a skinny kid from Arkansas
named Brooks Robinson who would later fill out, switch from second
base to third, and wind up in baseball's Hall of Fame.

"He was the best at making the play at second base that I ever
saw," said Gordon Kastner, catcher on the Corbitt Motors team. "I
know he saved me from many an error."

In basketball he captained the CBHS team his senior year while
playing guard, made first team all-Memphis, and finished seventh in
the city in scoring. The papers described him as "hard-driving and
almost impossible to stop." He could hit, run, shoot, and field, but
what old friends remember most about him was his determination
and fierce desire to win, and Lord have mercy on anyone who tried to

rough him up on the baseball diamond or the basketball court. They invariably describe him as "they kind of guy you wanted to have on your side."

Off the field he was shy and a good student. When he posed for the picture of the all-city basketball team, some girls came around to watch. "The photographers didn't need to use any flashbulbs," recalled teammate Don McCaskill. "Charlie's face was red enough to light up the whole room."

He had a temper. But when he got mad, often as not it was mad at himself if he felt he was letting the team down. Then one of his friends would go over and put an arm around him and calm him down. But it was always there. His senior year, Christian Brothers baseball coach Lew Chandler kicked him off the team until the other players voted to let him back on. The loyalty was characteristic of a team that had known each other since they were little kids. On a roster studded with Italians, he was listed in the program as Dago Tiller, 2nd base.

"It was a disciplinary thing," recalled Chandler. "I had told him to do something and he wouldn't do it. But after that things went smooth, and it was always yes sir and no sir. He was a good boy."

Boys in Memphis fought more then. White boys still fought in Golden Gloves. John Bramlett, a linebacker for the University of Memphis football team in the early sixties, was known as a brawler who made it all the way to the pros. Beyond that, the city had a general reputation for fighting for the hell of it at dances, parties, and clubs in the 1950s and 1960s. Charlie Torti, Tiller's teammate in basketball and baseball, was one of his best friends and enjoyed a scrap himself.

"Dago didn't cuss or smart off and he was just a whiz as a student. I only remember one fight he had in high school. You know how there's some kids in every school who are weak. Well, a new kid came over to Christian Brothers and was bullying this group. I was looking for him because these kids were my friends and I was going to beat him up. But Dago beat me to it. He found him first and whipped his butt proper."

After that championship season followed by senior year and graduation, the teammates broke up and went separate ways. Gordon Kastner went to college to study chemistry. Charlie Torti became a cop. Tiller's close friend John Howser went to medical school and became a neurosurgeon. Tiller also planned to go to medical school, but first wanted to give professional baseball a shot. He signed a Class D contract with Paducah of the old Kitty League but, the story goes, got mad one day and slugged his manager and that was the end of that. He would later explain that "I didn't hit my manager but I did hit just about every other son of a bitch."

He returned to Memphis and enrolled at Memphis State. Baseball and basketball were over, but he found a new sport he was good at — boxing. In 1957 he won a city Golden Gloves championship in the welterweight division. He might have gone further but he hated to train and preferred drinking beer and knocking heads in barrooms. He had started working out with weights and was up to a muscular 200 pounds, with a bull neck and biceps so big he could barely touch his shoulders. The newspapers began to report a string of arrests for fighting, drunkenness, and traffic charges. In 1962 he picked up his most serious charge to that point. A waitress he had dated said he smashed her face bloody then took her to a motel in Mississippi and sexually assaulted her. There was a second charge that year involving a fight at a drive-in. He failed to show up for his court appearance and skipped to California, fearful, he said later, that a jury would convict him and sentence him to 20 years or more.

In 1963 he got his first prison sentence — 18 months for two criminal assault charges. He vowed to turn his life around and "start working on being a decent person." But less than two years after completing his sentence he was back in trouble, charged with punching out a nightclub owner and throwing a table through a window. As they had years ago, some old friends from the neighborhood came to his aid. Billy Gray, an attorney, helped get him on work release, and David Goodwin, a developer, hired him on his construction crew.

It wasn't the kind of job he had planned on back at Christian Brothers but it wasn't bad either, with outdoor work and a regular paycheck. Goodwin, who had been Tiller's corner in Golden Gloves, liked his knack for learning how to read a set of plans and do estimating and was grooming him for supervisor. There was a fight or two but nothing unusual for construction work. Goodwin noticed he never had a problem with anyone trying to intimidate the supervisor. After a couple of years, Goodwin began getting out of home building and Tiller got restless and moved to California. People had begun to tell stories about his exploits. There was a legend that he had fought the UCLA football team. Years later, he explained that four UCLA players were sitting at a bar in Los Angeles and hit on his date.

"Some words were passed and I went to the car to get my baseball bat," he said. "I busted one upside the head and chased the other three outside the bar. When he woke up, he apologized to her. There is no truth to the other stories."

Charlie Torti went a different route after high school. He finished a couple years at Memphis State and then got married and had kids so he dropped out to go to work. Eventually he landed a job at the Police Department. He ran into Tiller a couple of times but lost touch with him. He read about his problems and didn't know what to make of them. But his old friend had changed, there wasn't any doubt about that. He knew the details of the crimes he was charged with, and they were worse than what had made the papers.

One night in the early sixties Tiller got into a fight at a joint called the Manhattan Club. It took five cops with nightsticks to get him cuffed and into a squad car. In those days, when a call went over the radio about a Tiller, a lot of cars answered it. Torti had hospital duty that night and was there when they brought Tiller in and dumped him on the floor. He was bleeding from the head, his hands were cuffed behind his back, and the cops had given him some pretty good pops. He looked up at his old friend and cried, "Charlie, take these ----ing cuffs off me and I'll beat the shit out of every one of them."

Torti made lieutenant in the West Precinct after a stint on the narcotics squad. A 1975 investigation of a California connection for amphetamine sales led back to Tiller. Reluctantly, he stayed on the investigation. He was doing surveillance on an apartment one night when suddenly detectives arrived at the house. A woman named Glenda Amos had been murdered. Shortly after that drug charges were filed against Tiller. There was no incident when he was arrested and they brought him downtown to get it straightened out. Torti was sitting in the police station shooting the breeze when a cop walked past who had once had a run-in with a girl Tiller knew. Suddenly his muscles tensed, his face turned red, and his eyes bulged out. It was like he was a different person from one second to the next.

Police and prosecutors called it a big drug operation. The California connection was an obese, invalid, elderly physician who supplied diet pills. Tiller was going to fight it. His reputation was too bad for there to be a slap on the wrist. But before the drug trial could come up he had bigger problems. In March of 1976 he was charged with the murders of Leroy Arrendale and Glenda Amos. Arrendale, a tough guy from Atlanta, had been shot three times with a shotgun in the parking lot of an apartment complex. Amos, his girlfriend, had been shot in the head with a 22-caliber pistol a few hours earlier at the apartment Torti had been staking out.

At first the police had two mystery murders on their hands. Soon they were able to put them together. Shortly after that they developed a suspect.

When Tiller saw the investigation leading to him he called an old friend from the Messick neighborhood, attorney Billy Gray. Gray was under federal indictment at the time for some business dealings, so the judge asked Tiller if he wanted another lawyer.

"Your honor," he said, "I would want Billy Gray for my lawyer if he were standing here in the same prison clothes as I am."

Gray stayed on.

"By and large it was a situation where I believed he was telling me the truth. I felt he had never told me anything but the truth, so I took the case. I had a great deal of hope and aspiration for Dago. He had some unfortunate things happen to him that he didn't have much control over that may have changed his thinking. There was a very suspicious charge against him that looked like it would prevent him from getting into medical school, and then his father died about the same time."

One of the attorneys opposing Gray was John Pierotti, a classmate of Tiller at Christian Brothers and a former colleague of Gray in the district attorney's office. In high school, Pierotti hung around with a different crowd. To Tiller, he was "one of those guys who played in the band or something." Actually, it was the Glee Club. After college and military service, he went to night law school and passed the bar exam and joined the D.A.'s office.

"I was the liaison to the homicide bureau. The investigation began as two mystery murders. There were no suspects at first. It was assigned to Joe Patterson, and Joe asked me for help since I was familiar with the investigation. Although I did know Charlie I just couldn't turn Joe down because nobody else had the knowledge of the thing that I did. I had some reluctance about it. I had known Charlie since the 9th grade, and I liked him. I remember him as a guy that was real popular with his classmates.

"Later I saw him from time to time when he had his problems up in criminal court. The last time I saw him he had gotten himself turned around and was working in construction. We had a class reunion somewhere along in there and I told several people how well I had heard Charlie was doing. When this thing broke, I had no idea Charlie had gotten himself back in trouble. Had it been a situation where somebody else wouldn't have had to do so much work, I'd have gotten off the case.

"If, as the proof showed, that Charlie did what he did, then I didn't feel that I owed him anything. If I tried the case Charlie was going to get a fair shake from me and the judge was going to give him a square shake because of his notoriety. It was a difficult case. Joe and I stopped everything we were doing and worked on the preparation for about three or four months. We spent a lot of time just trying to find people. In this kind of thing, the people that really know something are reluctant to talk to you. People were scared. I'm sure they felt that if he got off he might come and see them."

The key witness was a Vietnam special forces veteran named Jimmy Darden who had an apartment near the scene of the Arrendale killing. He and Tiller glared at each other during much of his testimony. Once one of Tiller's attorneys asked him how he could tell which of the three shots he heard had been the death shot. Darden rose up and confronted the lawyer. He said he knew what it sounded like when you put a gun next to someone's head and pulled the trigger because he had done it himself in Vietnam.

Tiller was convicted after four and a half hours of jury deliberations. He had turned down a deal of 20 years in exchange for a guilty plea. As the verdict was read, he stared at the jury and shook his head back and forth. He was sentenced to the state prison at Nashville then transferred to the maximum security prison at Brushy Mountain. He told Glen Sisson, one of his lawyers, that was OK with him. Brushy Mountain was where all the tough guys went.

When I wrote to Tiller, he asked cynically if I was "one of those crusading reporters." I told him I didn't have the crusading itch and firmly believed he was guilty. He agreed to see me anyway, but it took some time. He was inmate 79855. I got letters from him, always with that number in the return address, from Nashville, Brushy Mountain, and Fort Pillow. More than once, interviews had to be canceled because he was on administrative segregation.

He had been in prison for nine years when I came to see him in Nashville, where he had just been moved. A clerk gave me his visitors card and cleared me into the waiting area. He didn't get many visitors other than his mother, a small devout widow of whom he spoke reverently. A few minutes later a guard took the card and motioned for me to take a seat while he picked up the intercom to page Tiller. I recognized him from his pictures and got up to shake hands. He had on a baggy white jump suit and had just finished his seven-hour shift washing pots and pans in the prison kitchen. You had to take a dirty job, he explained, if you wanted to get a cushy one later on. Besides, potwasher paid $55 a month. He was planning on getting the recreation job he had at Brushy Mountain and Fort Pillow or, if he played his cards right, the easiest job in the joint — movie projectionist.

His hair is thinning and he has put on some weight around the middle, but his arms and shoulders look as stout as dock ropes. In his letters he said he had been on lock-up, but he was tanned and healthy as a construction worker. He wanted to know if I had heard why he had been moved again to Nashville.

"Just when you get used to a place, they move you again. But this is OK. There's a lot of guys I know here."

He talked about the old days.

"I wanted to be the toughest guy in Memphis then," he said. I said I had read that he was one of the toughest men in prison, reputedly the leader of a white gang. He had heard that and said it was bullshit. Black guys and white guys got along all right. It was the snitches and child molesters he couldn't stand. He talked about his infamous Tiller cousins, dismissing Michael and Albert but clearly fond of George, whom he called "a fightin' son of a bitch." We talked about sports. He lifts weights but doesn't play basketball or baseball any more. The young kids, he said, were all hotheads. All they want to do is argue. Stonney Lane, the warden at Brushy Mountain, said Tiller would sometimes act as umpire for inmate softball games, dispensing swift and certain justice on a field of broken dreams in the shadows of the East Tennessee mountains.

He is a closely watched inmate and knows it. The convict code, he said proudly, is not dead, but 90 percent of the men in prison don't live by it; the 10 percent that do are the only ones who deserve to be called convicts rather than inmates.

"Prison is like a jungle where you got lions and monkeys — and the monkeys don't get nothin" said the sly, tough old con who, at 48, is one of the oldest men in a population that is mostly young blacks. So he keeps at the weights and the mindless labor of the prison yard.

No one really knows for sure why he threw it all away and wound up where he did. He said he isn't sure himself. Maybe it had something to do with the fading of youth and what the psychologists call positive outlets, and a no-nonsense coach and teachers and a teammate to put a hand on his shoulder and calm him down. Maybe it was the notoriety or the burden of being the toughest man in Memphis or the death of his father or alcohol. Maybe it wasn't any of those things. Maybe it was just one of those strange changes of course in a life that leave you shaking your head with disappointment and wondering why.

The bishop of Nashville foresaw such things when he wrote to the CBHS Class of 1954. Mary, you see, was also the mother of sorrows.

Fight Night
at Ellis Auditorium
(Memphis, 1999)

River towns are usually tough towns, and Memphis in the 1950s was known for its fighters, whether on the streets and drive-ins or in the Golden Gloves competition at Ellis Auditorium. John Shepherd was a bouncer and heavyweight boxer from Whitehaven. He later had a successful career as a real estate appraiser but his true love is history. He has a phenomenal memory for names and dates and an encyclopedic store of tidbits of Memphis history like this one.

Fight Night
at Ellis Auditorium

The Golden Gloves boxing scene basically picked up after World War II until the late Fifties. There was a big sectional rivalry between South Memphis, which was based at the Gaston Community Center, and North Memphis, which was based at the Dave Wells Community Center. The City Finals and the Mid-South Golden Gloves, the last stop before the nationals in Chicago, were held at Ellis Auditorium.

No Memphian ever went all the way, but there were some good fighters. A guy named Irving "Tick-Tock" Tucker was a runner-up one year, and so was Billy Ray Smith, who went on to play football for the University of Arkansas and the Los Angeles Rams, and a guy named Sonny Ingram wore golden shoes and went to the semis. Of course it was completely segregated even though blacks and whites fought each other in the pros.

Most people just wanted to win a South Memphis or North Memphis Golden Gloves jacket, with that big golden glove on the back. You also got a little golden glove you could wear on your key chain, which was a big deal back then. So you had some pretty heated fights.

On the weekends there would be 1,200 to 1,400 people in the crowd in the early rounds and as many as 4,000 at Ellis Auditorium. Sometimes you would fight two or three times a night. The fights were only three rounds but they each seemed like two years. If each minute were that long in life you'd think you were Methuselah. People were full of vinegar after the war, and you had a lot of macho spirit. It was kind of the World Wrestling Federation of its day. There was a lot of blood and mouthpieces flying out into the audience. I saw a guy knock his opponent's mouthpiece almost to the state line one time. It was a real proving ground.

I played football and threw the shot put at Whitehaven High School. When I was 17 my brother got me a job as a bouncer at The Peabody. I also worked as a bouncer at the Cotton Club and Danny's in West Memphis. The country club set went to the Plantation Inn. I was a good bouncer because I couldn't drink and I couldn't dance. The Peabody was nothing rough because they only let couples come in. It was one of only a few places in Memphis that Mr. Crump allowed to have a dance permit. I guess he thought that dancing let good people act bad. That drove the rougher crowd to the Cotton Club and Danny's in West Memphis, where you could go stag. Bouncers carried a flashlight, and if you flashed it on the ceiling the other bouncers would come running and help break up the fight and throw the guys out. Memphis was actually a pretty safe town then because everybody didn't have guns and knives and Mr. Crump had a tough police force.

Most of the street fights were at the drive-ins. Cars were scarce, so you had four or five people in a car, and each school or neighborhood had its favorite hangout like Leonard's Barbecue, Beretta's, the Pig and Whistle, Gray's, or K's. You didn't go through another school's drive-in unless you were willing to put your jaw on the line.

A great street fighter isn't necessarily a good boxer. The best ones trained the hardest and had discipline. I fought as a heavyweight and won the South Memphis championship but got beat in the city finals by George Tiller, one of the Tiller brothers who became sort of famous for getting into trouble. We were the same age but he was three grades behind me in school. Both of us later joined the Marine Corps, and our serial numbers were one digit apart. George got thrown out after Parris Island, and he told his drill instructors, "If you think I'm bad, wait until Shepherd gets here."

After the D.I. told me that, I was a model Marine. I didn't miss a march step.

The First Family
of Memphis Jockdom
(Memphis, 1998*)*

Canale Family

The all-around athlete is a vanishing breed, but in the Fifties
and Sixties, the Canale family produced six brothers, all of whom played
college football at Tennessee or Mississippi State. Justin and Whit played
professional football until knee injuries ended their careers. Their cousin,
Dr. Terry Canale, is a leading orthopedic surgeon at the Campbell Clinic
in Germantown and performed several of their operations.

The First Family
of Memphis Jockdom

They don't make big guys like they used to. Or break them down either, thank goodness. Consider Justin Canale: 55 years old, 16 years of college and professional football behind him, and an operation for every year plus a few to spare.

When Canale was growing up in Memphis in the 1950s and 1960s, his weight room was his father's farm in Germantown or a Sinclair gas station on Union Avenue. His weights were hay bales, drain pipes and car axles if there weren't any barbells around, or muscle-against-muscle "dynamic tension" as it was known in the comic book vernacular of the time. One summer he strengthened his arms and shoulders by repeatedly lifting a young calf, giving new meaning to the term free weights. He stopped for fear of injury — to the cow, of course.

His personal trainers were a swarm of equally robust brothers and cousins. The Canales were Memphis' First Family of Jockdom. Brothers Frank, George, Billy, Whit, Justin, and Conn all starred at either Christian Brothers High School or Memphis Catholic and later played Southeastern Conference (SEC) football. Throw in their cousins from the same era — Terry Canale, who played linebacker at Virginia, and the four Tagg brothers — and you had a football team that could have lined up against Ole Miss without going outside of the family gene pool.

All six Canale brothers were within a year or two of the next sibling.

"It seems like every year our folks went over to Hot Springs and came back and Mother would be pregnant," said Justin.

In 1964, a writer for *Sports Illustrated* aptly described the family farm with its ball fields, shot put pit, and hurdles as a gladiatorial training ground. The brothers' inter-family football games at Crump Stadium were legendary. So were meal times, when Mama Canale would lay on platters of ham, fried chicken, potatoes and gravy, and biscuits.

"It was survival of the fittest," said Terry. "Whoever was the biggest guy got the most, except for Frank who was the oldest and easily the meanest."

You can still get a debate over who was the best all-around athlete. Justin said Whit, a Mickey Mantle-style mesomorph who ran the hundred-yard dash in under 10 seconds, threw the shot put, broad-jumped, and played fullback and end for Tennessee before knee injuries ended his career. Terry said it was George, who starred at tailback for the Vols and still holds the school record for most average rushing yardage per carry.

For size and strength, Justin was the one. He was what some people call farm-boy strong. "Weight lifting for football players was just getting started," he said of his youth. "You'd just grab it, pick it up, see who could lift the most weight, and that was it." He could pick up a basketball and squeeze it until it popped. Long after his football career was over, he was still one of the most powerful-looking men in Memphis, with enormous forearms and shoulders, and also one of the gentlest and kindest.

He threw the shot put 58 feet in college, good enough to win the SEC championship. He played offensive and defensive guard for Mississippi State, chasing, among others, a fleet quarterback from Alabama named Joe Willie Namath. He kicked 50-yard field goals in the old-fashioned, straight-on style. Then he played 12 years in pro football as a lineman and kicker with the Boston Patriots of the AFL, the Cincinnati Bengals of the NFL, the Montreal Alouettes and the Calgary Stampeders of the Canadian Football League, and the Memphis Grizzlies of the World Football League. That rare four-league tour is matched by one other statistic: at least 20 operations due to football injuries.

Justin still looks capable of moving defensive linemen around. Then you wince as he tries to sit down. He has phlebitis, gout, lower back pain, one missing kneecap, no knee cartilage, and no circulation in his lower legs, which are the color of grape juice. Anti-inflammatory drugs burned a hole in his intestines. He is, according to a doctor's statement in his thick medical file, "capable of sedentary work only" and unable to play sports. He and brother Conn own Canale's Grocery at a country crossroads in Eads that serves hundreds of smoked-ham sandwiches every day to construction workers.

Justin's medical condition is due partly to the violent nature of his former occupation and partly to the warrior's code and rehabilitation practices of his day. "If you couldn't play and produce they didn't have time for you," he said. He was healthy through high school and most of college, when he still competed in both football and track and field. His weight varied from 245 to 265 pounds, smaller than many high school linemen today. His knees began to go midway through his pro career, following a serious groin pull suffered in a one-on-one practice drill. Cortisone injections and the surgeon's knife kept him in the game and prolonged his career but ultimately made him a near cripple.

"A guy like Justin probably played when he shouldn't have played," said Terry, an orthopedic surgeon at Campbell Clinic and longtime team physician for the University of Memphis football team. Terry did three of Justin's operations. "Things happened that shouldn't have happened."

If Justin is the Incredible Hulk, Terry is the Incredible Shrinking Man. When he played linebacker for Virginia in 1958-1962, he weighed 220 pounds. In medical school, he dropped down to 190 pounds. Fifteen years ago, he began a serious running program, combined with tennis and swimming, and now weighs 165 pounds, or about what he weighed in junior high school. His only overdeveloped muscle is his heart, with a pulse rate that been measured as low as 40.

The impetus for his training regimen is what happened to his father. Sturla Canale, a football star at Notre Dame under Knute Rockne, died on a handball court in 1957 at the age of 47. He was several pounds overweight, wearing a rubber sweat suit, and bucking a family history of heart disease. As a result, Terry has devoted a considerable part of his personal and professional life to physical fitness.

Not that he was injury-free himself. He counts two shoulder separa-
tions, a nose broken several times, a broken elbow, and a broken ankle
from football.

"We once calculated that if you played one year of college football, your chances of significant injury were 30 to 40 percent. If you
played four years, your chances were 110 percent."

Every year now for several years, there is a Canale family reunion
at Canale Farms in Fayette County. Drew Canale, a cousin of Justin,
Whit, and Terry, got into the reunion business when the market for
riding horses dried up after actor Chrisopher Reeves' accident left
"Superman" paralyzed. The old jocks get together to tell stories, look
at pictures, and eat picnic-style the way they used to. Once they were
gridiron stars, and they have the scars to prove it.

VII.
Souvenirs of a Journalist

Gordon Kahl's Ozark Odyssey

(Mid-South magazine, 1983)

Gordon Kahl

Gordon Kahl was a fugitive who had already killed two federal agents and sworn he wouldn't be taken alive. Gene Mathews was the sheriff of Lawrence County, Arkansas, and not the sort of man to take orders, even from FBI agents. In 1983, Kahl's flight from North Dakota brought him to Lawrence County, 100 miles west of Memphis, where the deadly shootout was more dramatic than either man could have imagined. Kahl was the forerunner of Oklahoma City bomber Timothy McVeigh and David Koresh and the Branch Davidians. He was patriotic and religious but bigoted and fanatical in his hatred of the federal government. Arkansas was a haven for tax protesters, survivalists, and hate groups in the 1980s. Two years after Kahl was killed, a survivalist named James Ellison and his well-armed band of followers engaged in a tense standoff with federal agents near Bull Shoals Lake before surrendering. A young prosecutor intimately familiar with both cases was Asa Hutchinson of Fort Smith, now Under Secretary of the Department of Homeland Security.

Gordon Kahl's Ozark Odyssey

For more than 10 years Gordon Wendell Kahl had been playing cat and mouse with the IRS and the U.S. Marshal's office.
In Texas, North Dakota and Arkansas, nobody knew quite
what to make of this middle-aged farmer who refused to pay income
taxes or register his cars, took his kids out of school, set up his own
church, hated Jews, didn't believe in paper money and belonged to
something called the Posse Comitatus.

He was a real puzzle: a hard-working family man, a World War II
veteran and a crack mechanic, but on the subject of taxes the guy was
just about at the end of his rope. Things kept escalating. The IRS got
him into court in Texas on probation, but a couple years later he moved
to North Dakota and it started all over again. Once he chased IRS
agents away from his house with a shotgun. In 1981 he just disappeared.
The federal government confiscated 80 acres of his farmland last fall
and sold it to pay taxes.

It was a ticklish problem for the IRS. Many tax protesters were,
like Kahl, WASPs and members of the geriatric set who had served
their country and led hard-working, more or less normal lives. If you
didn't see the undercurrent of bigotry and fanaticism in their movement,
they could generate a lot of sympathy in Middle America. Everybody
griped about taxes, and most people cut corners wherever they could.
And the number of protesters was growing. Although it was nowhere
near the millions the Posse claimed, there were about 40,000 hardcore

protesters, nearly quadruple the number there were three years ago, even by IRS estimates. The agency was determined not to let Kahl and others flaunt their resistance and get away with it.

The fact that a lot of protesters had short fuses only compounded the problem. The people that had to deal with them were U.S. marshals. Despite the archaic connotation, marshals are basically process servers, not Wild West-style gunslingers. If they ever cornered someone like Kahl, there could be a hell of a lot of trouble.

By February of this year, Kahl was back with his family in North Dakota, living openly for the last two months, his neighbors said. The meeting he had organized for Feb. 13 in Medina was vintage Posse. The little group planned to set up a new "township" based on common law and the Third Continental Congress. Posse members also jealously claim their rights under, among others, the Magna Charta, the Northwest Ordinance of 1789 and the Articles of Confederation. Once a "sovereign" township was established, they would proceed to elect officers and sue everyone they don't like.

Their business completed, they headed for home. Kahl and Dave Broer were in one car; Yorie Kahl, Joan Kahl, Scott Faul and Vernon Wegner were in another. Kahl, Yorie, Broer and Faul were armed with guns, which is not unusual for Posse members (a favorite saying is "There is no greater law firm than Smith & Wesson especially when it is backed by a 12-gauge injunction"). Kahl even went to the dinner table with his mini-14, a semiautomatic rifle that is a civilian version of the military's M-14.

As they came over a hill north of Medina they saw a roadblock and two police cars several hundred yards in the distance. The vehicle carrying the Kahls pulled off into a driveway that led to a trailer home. A third police vehicle roared up behind them to block their retreat. Kahl, Yorie and Scott Faul climbed out of their cars, weapons drawn. The marshals told them to drop their guns and said they had a warrant to arrest Kahl for violation of his probation. There was a loud argument as the standoff lasted nearly 10 minutes. Suddenly there was a burst of gunfire from Yorie Kahl's direction, then bedlam.

When the smoke cleared a minute later, two marshals lay dead and three other officers were wounded, along with Yorie Kahl. Gordon and Scott loaded Yorie into a police car and sped away to a nearby clinic. After dropping him off, they fled. The two men spent that night near Harvey, N.D. Faul, only 29 and a newcomer to the Posse, decided to turn himself in. But there would be no surrender for Gordon Kahl. The ultimate paranoiac, he now saw his visions coming true. He had shot five lawmen, killing at least two of them. He had seen his son shot, perhaps mortally wounded for all he knew. Every lawman in North Dakota would soon be looking for him. The feds had always been out to get him anyway, ever since he stopped paying income tax in 1969. It was time to go underground again. He penned a quick note on the back of a feed sack, taking full responsibility for shooting the marshals and exonerating the others. He left the note with Faul. Then he disappeared into the fog of the chilly North Dakota night.

Two days later several heavily-armed lawmen raided Kahl's farmhouse near Heaton, N.D. They found a cache of weapons and ammunition and 14 gas masks but no trace of Kahl. But officers would remember this mini arsenal when they cornered Kahl three and a half months later.

The next day authorities received a second message from Kahl, this time a letter which described in detail his version of the shoot-out. "While urgency, or human weakness, tells me to run, my spirit said write, so this I am going to do and if my God continues to protect me, I shall write first, and flee from the hands of my enemies later." In the long account, peppered with anti-Semitic references, he again took full responsibility for shooting the marshals, who he claimed opened fire on his son first. He describes how, one by one, he "took them out of the fight" with is mini-14. Government attorneys would later show that the marshals also were fired on by Yorie Kahl and Scott Faul, both convicted of second-degree murder in U.S. District Court in May.

"I must now depart," the letter concluded. "I have no idea where I'm going. But after some more prayer, I will go where the Lord leads me and either live to carry on the fight or die, if that be the case."

A day later the U.S. Marshal's Service issued wanted posters for Gordon Kahl and offered a $25,000 reward.

The Lord led him to northern Arkansas in late February. First he stopped in Texas, where he chopped up and buried his car, then just over the state line in Mena, Ark., where he had hidden out a year earlier before his fateful return to North Dakota. But they would be looking for him there, and he moved on.

There were practical as well as biblical reasons why the trail of a man like Gordon Kahl might lead to the Ozark foothills. The Ozarks had long been popular with retirees, some of whom found right-wing causes more diverting than mountain scenery. With its rugged terrain and cheap, fairly inaccessible land, the area had become something of a haven for survivalists and right wingers of all stripes. When The Bomb went off, or the Commies came up the Mississippi, or the sinful cities went the way of Sodom and Gomorrah, a man might fall back on his wits, his guns and his family and stand a chance in the Ozarks.

At least that's what Leonard Ginter believed. In 1977 he left Wisconsin, where he was active in the Posse, for Arkansas. He settled in Lawrence County on a little piece of land owned by Bill Wade, a model farmer turned tax protester. Ginter built himself a little dugout house and planted a big garden in a pretty hollow alongside a creek. The house wasn't much more than some concrete walls built into the side of a hill, with dirt bulldozed over the top. But it was cozy, energy-efficient and hidden.

Like Kahl, Ginter was in his early 60s, mechanically minded, paranoid and soured on civilization. He burned with an itch to sue all the judges and politicians who were ruining things, and sue them he did. Judge Harry Ponder of Lawrence County and District Attorney Emil Everix of his old home county of western Wisconsin were two of his favorite demons, and he regularly bombarded them with hand-typed briefs demanding his rights under the Holy Bible, Magna Charta and the Northwest Ordinance. Ponder kept them in a file under the heading "Strange Pleadings."

While in Wisconsin, Ginter became acquainted with one James Wickstrom, the self-styled leader of the Posse Comitatus who put members on "standby alert" following the Medina shooting. Wickstrom was in contact with Kahl during his flight and offered to negotiate his surrender. The Posse, despite its grandiose claims, is by more scientific estimates a small group of hard-core rebels whose members keep abreast of one another. Federal authorities are still investigating suspects who may have aided Kahl's flight, but it would not have been at al unlikely for Wickstrom to have put Kahl in touch with Ginter if they did not already know each other.

"I remember when I heard on the radio that Kahl had been shot some place in Arkansas, the first thing I thought of was Leonard," recalls Everix.

Kahl spent a day or two with Ginter and his wife in late February before he moved again. Why he moved is uncertain. Perhaps they felt that Ginter and Wade, both active in a local tax protest group and occasionally in court on various legal disputes, kept too high a profile. The IRS was watching the Lawrence County tax protesters. Agents had seized a truck belonging to one of them, Cleo Denison, and they had hauled Buck Stewart, of nearby Lynn off to prison. But Ginter had friends in western Arkansas who were also Posse members and Identity Christians (a bitterly anti-Semitic movement popular with the Radical Right). The location was also as remote, the company equally trustworthy (or so they thought) and there seemed less chance of recognition or betrayal. So they took the fugitive to Baxter County, 80 miles to the west.

Ed Udey, 70, had settled in Baxter County in 1974, coming back to his native state after a long and distinguished career as a photographer. Educated in botany and entomology at the University of Arkansas, he landed a job as a cameraman for the Marines in World War II, making medical films of the treatment of battle wounds in the South Pacific. After the war he was part of a top-secret crew that filmed the development and testing of the atomic and hydrogen bombs. He has some 30 skin cancer scars on his face that may have been caused by exposure to radiation at the test sites. Later he did television commercials, nature and animal photography around the world and worked with Marlin Perkins on the program "Wild Kingdom."

By the 1970s, Udey thought the country was going to hell. Foreign aid to the Communists. Grain to Russia. The giveaway of the Panama Canal. Humanism. Inflation. Moral decay. Taxes and the damned IRS eating away at your life's work. Even in Cotter they were after you. An avid reader, he found answers in the Bible — he keeps dozens of them — the doomsday literature, the eat-right-for-health cult and the polemics of the Radical Right — especially the Posse, the Identity Movement and the tax protesters. He challenged the IRS from 1975 on and led Identity meetings at a room in the sheriff's office in nearby Mountain Home.

When Leonard Ginter told him about Gordon Kahl, it wasn't hard for him to sympathize with the fugitive. Kahl was something of a hero. It would be an honor, a patriot's duty to assist him. The problem was that Udey and his wife lived practically in the middle of Cotter, a short block off U.S. 62, and like Ginter, he kept a high public profile. He suspected his telephone was being tapped and his mail was being tampered with. It would be better for Kahl to stay somewhere else, some place more isolated, with someone less active on the Radical Right. Someone like Arthur Russell in Mountain Home.

The 74-year-old Russell lived on 11 acres off Arkansas 178 a mile out of town where the road heads off toward the hills. Recently widowed, he had raised 10 children and worked practically every day of his adult life. He had a reputation as a top-notch well driller and pump repairman. Anything he did had to be done perfect or it just wasn't done, people who knew him said.

Like Udey, Russell grew increasingly bitter in the 1970s. He filed 5th Amendment income tax returns (a discredited tax dodge) after 1972. In 1978 he served 29 days in jail for willful failure to pay income taxes. About the same time he broke with the local Mormon Church when the church hierarchy extended privileges of the priesthood to blacks. "That nigger bit," he called it. He became an Identity Christian. He called Jews "the children of Satan" and railed against "the Jew bastard, son of a bitch doctor" who gave his wife an anesthetic known as twilight sleep during her last pregnancy.

Russell lived alone after his wife died two years ago. Her funeral was the only time he ever saw all 10 of his children at once. They posed for pictures that afternoon, proud old Arthur and his tribe grinning before Ed Udey's camera. Then the children scattered once again, and he went back to his wells, his garden and his tax protests. When he wasn't working he spent his time reading the Bible or licking envelopes late into the night for pyramid-style, get-rich-quick schemes someone would talk him into now and then.

But when Leonard Ginter and Gordon Kahl arrived at Arthur Russell's house on a Sunday morning in late February, they found three other occupants along with the old man. Twenty-eight year old Karen Elaine Robertson, Arthur's youngest child, had moved in two months earlier. She had recently been divorced from her husband in Oklahoma, and Arthur had fetched her and her two little girls and brought them home.

Karen had just returned from church when her father asked her to come into the kitchen. He made her promise she would not say anything about anybody who was staying in the house or anything that was said for a time. Then a man walked out of the bedroom. Her father introduced him as Gordon Kahl. Karen asked if he had really killed those two federal marshals in North Dakota, and Kahl said he had. But she must never say anything to anyone, the men told her again. Or else. Karen understood. She felt if she said anything she would be killed. Kahl told her she should call him Sam Louden (the name he had used two years ago when he lived in Mena). Arthur would call him Curly. Then he introduced himself to Karen's 8- and 4-year-old daughters. He told them he was very popular and a lot of people wanted to see him. The kids, well, they could just call him Uncle Sam.

Uncle Sam wasn't a bad sort of fella once you got over being afraid of him. He was good with children and the girls liked him, and Karen found him likable enough. He helped with the cooking and made out the grocery lists. Or he watched television or read, mostly the Bible but some of Arthur's books too, like Flee to the Mountains, Jacob's Pillar and The Late Great Planet Earth. Occasionally the Udeys would come over for dinner or Arthur and Gordon would go over there.

But other times he could scare you to death. He and Udey and Ginter were so secretive, communicating only in person. But Karen heard things. Kahl was determined to get back to North Dakota to get revenge for the shoot-out in Medina and for a friend he believed had been punished for refusing to help authorities. There were at least two sheriffs, a deputy and a chief of police he vowed he would kill. He liked to draw a little bit too. In particular Karen remembered a crazy-looking thing that was supposed to be the seven-headed beast in the

Book of Revelation. It mocked several races and religions but mainly
the Jews and the Masons. Sometimes Gordon would brag about the
$25,000 reward on his head or about his guns. He had a mini-14, a
pistol and a rifle with a high-powered night scope on it. Once he
showed her the rifle and pointed it toward the window. She looked
through the sight. It made a tree way out in the pasture look like you
could reach out and touch it.

In May Karen began to hear whisperings that the FBI was closing
in. Around the middle of the month Ginter and his wife made another
visit accompanied by another man introduced as Bill Wade (the owner
of the farm in Smithville on which Ginter's house is located). Ginter
and Udey came to the house again on May 30, Memorial Day. Karen
was outside unloading her pickup truck. By the time she finished they
were gone, and so was Gordon Kahl. The next day she called the FBI.

The FBI in Little Rock put her in touch with special agent Jack
Knox, who came to Mountain Home June 1. They met at a park at 7
p.m. Karen was supposed to be at church. She was so nervous she
couldn't remember his name, but she gradually put together the whole
story of Kahl's three-month stay. They agreed to use the names Fort
Knox and Mercy in future conversations.

"If my name gets out in the open, I'm dead. So are my kids,"
Karen told him.

Knox tried to reassure her. She would be relocated and given a
new identity and at least $15,000 in reward money.

"Go slow, and everything's gonna be OK," he told her.

"I'm scared to death is what I am. It's just the thought if them
getting my kids... they, they kind of hinted around that if they didn't
kill me and the kids then they'd see to it that the FBI did... I'm kind
of scared to stay there at the house now."

"Well, nothing's going to get out on this."

"Because I'm scared to death that my father, I, sometimes he is
the sanest man in the world and other times he just acts kind of crazy
and I'm scared of him. And if I would have had a job I would have
been out by now."

"Well, we're not gonna do anything that's gonna cause you or the
kids any harm. We're gonna go slow. The main thing is to try to appre-
hend Gordon without any incident. That's what our purpose is."

The FBI put Ginter's house under aerial surveillance after Karen Russell's information was received. They would be extremely cautious given Kahl's history, his vow not to be taken alive, the threats of revenge and the ammunition and weapons found at his farm in North Dakota.

In the late afternoon of June 3, FBI agents, Lawrence County Sheriff's officers, U.S. marshals and Arkansas State Police moved in on the Ginter house. As they closed in they met Leonard Ginter driving away from the house. He had a cocked, loaded pistol in his lap and a rifle on the seat nearby. Ginter was ordered out of the vehicle and asked if there were anyone else inside. He said only his wife, and called to her, "Norma, come on out, it's the FBI."

Mrs. Ginter came out of the house and joined the little group, which included FBI Special Agent In Charge Jim Blasingame, Arkansas State Police investigator Ed Fitzpatrick, U.S. marshal Jim Hall and Sheriff Gene Matthews. As they stood talking, Matthews went on into the house. Fellow officers would later say he was not the sort of man who waited for others to take the lead. Inside the kitchen he came face to face with Gordon Kahl. For one apocalyptic instant they looked at each other, then they fired. Matthews was struck in the side, between the front and the back of his bulletproof vest. Kahl was hit in the head.

Seconds later a lawman pumped a shotgun blast through a window. It struck Matthews in the back. He staggered outside and gasped, "I got him" as tear gas and arms fire rang out from all directions, setting off a fire in the house which ignited thousands of rounds of ammunition. The sheriff would die three hours later at the hospital from loss of blood. It was several hours before the explosions stopped and the fire died down and they recovered the charred remains of Gordon Kahl.

On June 4 Leonard and Norma Ginter were charged by the state with capital murder. Nearly three weeks later, June 21, the Ginters, along with Ed and Irene Udey and Arthur Russell, were charged by a federal grand jury in Fort Smith, Ark. with conspiracy to harbor the fugitive, Gordon Kahl. The clerk thanked them for coming over to testify then laid the indictments right on top of their travel expense checks. As soon as Arthur Russell read it, he knew who the informant had been.

Karen Elaine Robertson left Mountain View June 22, the day after her father went to Fort Smith. She has since been relocated and given a new identity by the FBI. It is unlikely she will ever see her father again. Asked about his daughter, Arthur Russell said recently, "That lyin' daughter of mine is the only witness they've got. She was the tail end of the 10 kids and was always just a spoiled brat. That's our good government for you. They take people and get 'em to spill their guts and then they give 'em protection and a new identity. They tried to get me to fess up and do all this goody-goody stuff and lay it all on everybody else, but it didn't work. I'm just not that kind of person."

On Oct. 11 in federal court in Harrison, Ark., the Udeys, the Ginters and Arthur Russell went on trial. A motley group of right-wing sympathizers attended each day of the one-week trial. Karen Robertson was the government's star witness. Through nearly five grueling hours of repetitive questioning, attorneys for the defendants were unable to shake her from her story. Arthur Russell, his hand cupping his ear, sat listening and shaking his head.

Irene Udey was acquitted the fifth day of the trial. The jury deliberated only two and a half hours before finding the other defendants guilty. On Nov. 29 Ed Udey and Leonard Ginter were sentenced to five years in prison. Arthur Russell received a five-year sentence with all but six months suspended. Norma Ginter was given a five-year suspended sentence. The Ginters still face state charges of murder in connection with the death of Gene Matthews, but the trial is not expected to begin until next year, assuming the charges are not dropped.

Gordon Kahl has not been forgotten. A group of sympathizers claims he was ambushed in Medina and murdered in Smithville and hacked into pieces. The latest theory holds that it was not really his body at all that was found in Ginter's house. A.J. Lowery, publisher of the tax-protest newspaper The Justice Times in Clinton, Ark., has devoted an entire issue to "Kahlgate." He plans to run for president on a tax-protest platform and has penned a song about Kahl called "Federal Fanatics":

> *Federal fanatics*
> *Came after Gordon Kahl*
> *Even though he never*

Broke any law at all.
Maniacs with a badge and a gun.
What would you do
If they gunned your son?
We gotta stop the antics
Of federal fanatics.
They're a menace to society
There's nothin' any worse
Than federal fanatics
'Cept maybe the K.G.B.

Ed Udey has shaved off the beard he wore during the trial and has resumed his quiet life in Cotter. He said he has more time to study the Bible and the Constitution now.

Arthur Russell lives alone once again, reading his Bible, doing his mailings and fixing a pump now and then. "See that book there," he said, pointing at a Bible. "I haven't found a place in it that said a man is supposed to stop earning a living by the sweat of his brow."

He managed to bring in a good crop of sweet potatoes for the winter, along with some Swiss chard, tomatoes and strawberries, but the garden isn't what it should be "'cuz at the time I was supposed to be doing somethin' they put me in the damn jug house."

The wind still blows through the crack in his door where agents busted in to execute their search warrant June 21. In addition to evidence they took several thousand dollars worth of silver coins and bullion he had stashed in an ammunition box in his bedroom.

"They gave it to the goddamned infernal revenue," he said. And he bends over in the little circle of light in the darkness to address another envelope.

William B. Tanner's Rise and Fall

(Mid-South magazine, 1985)

William B. Tanner

An offshoot of corporate scandals such as Enron, Arthur Andersen, and WorldCom was the "perp walk" where the FBI parades a handcuffed corporate executive accused of wrongdoing through a gauntlet of news cameras and reporters. The press gets to shout questions which the perp walker ignores before ducking into a government car. William B. Tanner is probably the most famous perp walker in Memphis history. He didn't take a perp walk. He ran a perp marathon, starting with the autumn afternoon in 1983 when the FBI raided his office with a show of force worthy of a drug raid. The William B. Tanner Company was in the advertising, media buying, and barter business. Tanner was convicted of tax evasion and served 18 months in a federal prison. I got to know him well, and the phrases "no comment" and "you'll have to talk to my lawyer" simply were not in his vocabulary. From the day his office was raided until the day he was sentenced two years later, he did his own talking, for better or worse. His corporate crimes pale in comparison to those of recent offenders on Wall Street and in corporate suites. After doing his time, he started a successful outdoor advertising company, including most of the billboards between Memphis and Tunica. Almost unbelievably energetic and irrepressible, he has overcome cancer and now owns Kia car dealerships in Nashville.

William B. Tanner's Rise and Fall

"*He had a good dream. It's the only one you can have. To come out number-one man.*"
— Happy Loman in Arthur Miller's
Death of a Salesman

William B. Tanner has been wrestling with his ego all his life.

As a boy he could pick more cotton than most grown men in Portageville, Mo. As a young salesman he could sell more deodorant and more radio commercials than anybody. At 54, he now has more of everything — money, cars, clothes, parties and, lately, legal problems — than just about anyone in Memphis. He has, at various times in his career, been recognized for accomplishments in business, hair grooming, bridge, racquetball and philanthropy — and he has the clippings to prove it.

He speaks in superlatives. The William B. Tanner Company was "the biggest in the world" in the media barter industry. Its sale to Media General was "the sweetest deal ever made in the history of American companies." Harold Robbins, "the best-selling author in the country," has approached him about writing his story. He has recently been attending a Bible study class and, yes, the Bible is "the greatest book in the world."

On the other hand, when things haven't gone his way Tanner has been heard to complain loudly about "disgruntled" former employees,

blind racquetball referees, "abusive" police officers, "one-sided" newspapers, and "Gestapo tactics" by the IRS and FBI.

This is the blustering of an angry man and even Tanner knows
it. He was done in not so much by his enemies as by the flatterers and
bribe takers he thought served him well and, most of all, by his own
conniving. Fittingly, the investigation that landed him in prison started
in part of the offices of the William B. Tanner Company: an anonymous
letter full of wild allegations against a Lipton Company employee
started an investigation that eventually found its way to Memphis. If
Tanner hadn't finally hired some lawyers with the sense to say no to
him, he'd have fought to the last bullet and probably be looking at
more than four years.

But you will forget all this for a moment when you meet Tanner
in person. The first thing you notice is his voice — a nasal Bootheel
twang that would be at home in a palaver with Jerry Clower or Minnie
Pearl. He said "was" for "were" and has dropped more g's than Dizzy
Dean. When he tells a funny story, which he does often and well, usually aiming the humor at himself, he doesn't laugh, he giggles. It is the
one unmistakable trace of Portageville he still has, right there with all
the millions, the Churchill collection, the Stutz Blackhawk, the $800
suits, the razor haircuts, the mansion. There is still that voice from the
past: "Sellin' proprietary drugs, why I was just gettin' warmed up after
the third or fifth no."

Hey, you think, it's just Bill Boy Tanner from Portageville.

To get there you take Interstate 55 out of Memphis, through the
flatlands 110 miles to just over the Missouri line. Tanner's older sister,
Marjorie Riddick, still lives in Portageville. Like her brother she is
proud and self-confident. When the Memphis newspapers reported
the legal troubles of various family members, she was so mad she
bought up every copy in the racks in Portageville so no one else could
see them. "Once it cost me $13," she said.

She recalls her younger brother as an A and B student who was
good at basketball and softball, dressed well and was popular with the
girls. From the time they were old enough to start school, she and her
brother did odd jobs to earn spending money. Tanner swept out the
elementary school, worked in the family's little store, delivered groceries
and picked cotton.

"Bill could pick more cotton than anybody," she said. "Once he picked 400 pounds in a day."

Jewell Burgess, who taught Tanner and 56 other children in her fourth-grade class vouches for the story.

"He was outstanding even then, you could tell it. If there was any competition he was right up at the top."

The Tanners were middle class by Portageville standards in those Depression days, which now seem difficult indeed. The Rural Electrification Administration did not bring power to the Bootheel until nearly 1940. The little Tanner farmhouse had an outdoor bathroom and a refrigerator and washing machine powered by kerosene. Residents say Henry Tanner, known as "Hentan," and his wife Grace were compassionate, smart, strong-willed people who often disagreed. Although they died of cancer within a year of each other, they are buried in different sections of the local cemetery. "Hentan," a successful farmer and something of a force in Portageville politics in his later years, is buried under a tombstone second only to the town founder's in size. He wrote his own epitaph and his portrait is etched on the gravestone.

In that respect at least, Tanner took after his father. Mrs. Riddick, however, said her brother "has always been a momma's boy."

"My mother thought he hung the moon and he thought she did too," she said. It was their mother who named her son "Billy Boy" after the popular song. Tanner later had his name changed to William. Asked what his middle initial stands for, he jokes that it stands for "bad" then tells the story of his given name. "Can you believe someone being named Billy Boy?" he asks, shaking his head. Years ago he hung the same moniker on his own son.

After he made his fortune, Tanner occasionally came back to Portageville for Christmas or special events. A few years ago he gave the high school a new sound system for the gymnasium. Mayor Arvil Adams remembers the busload of friends — members of a Cotton Carnival society group — Tanner brought with him and the watches or cars he later gave away or sold to the Portageville police chief and others at bargain prices. "You can give all you want but you can't buy loyalty," Adams said. Not surprisingly, there was some snickering when Tanner's troubles were reported two years ago.

"You know human nature," said Adams. "Let somebody make something of himself and get out of here, and some people are gonna say he stole it. But I've also heard farmers say, 'I don't care if he did wrong, at least he did something.'"

That he did. After high school it didn't take Tanner long to decide he wasn't going to hang around Portageville. He went to Southwest Missouri Junior College then on to the University of Missouri for two years, paying his way by selling liquor and corsages to the fraternity boys, making a dollar on each one. "It was a hell of a deal," he recalls fondly. He says that a lot.

After two years at Missouri — he never bothered to graduate — he came back to Portageville and tried his hand at farming and selling fertilizer. But country life didn't suit him. An early marriage to a Bootheel girl ended in divorce. He tried selling movie rights but quit when he discovered the theater owners were sandbagging him on the house count. Following a stint in the Air Force, he was smitten by another one of his now frequent brainstorms for the manufacture of a little electric car for kids which he dubbed the Futurama Jet.

"Futurama was the name of a lipstick company then and jet was for the start of the jet age. Pretty good huh?"

The 23-year-old inventor built his prototype and towed it all the way to the New York Toy Show in a $119 trailer, sleeping in truck stops and staying at some dump in New York. The buyers loved it and he went back to Missouri with over $100,000 worth of orders in the pockets of his jeans. But the Futurama Jet never got into big-time production and, after an aborted overture from Pontiac Motors ("just tryin' to pick my brain") the company went bankrupt. Soured on Missouri, sick of farming and itching to get ahead, he packed up his car and headed south on U.S. 61 to Memphis.

He wound up getting a job as a salesman with Berjon Company, a little patent medicine business. Recalling those days, Tanner launches into one of his country-fried Horatio Alger stories: Berjon sent him to the Mississippi Delta with one of its veteran salesmen to get trained for five days. The veteran, it seems, was enjoying the nocturnal favors of a young lady from Meridian and ordered Tanner to meet him in the coffee shop at 11 a.m. — an immensely late hour for an eager beaver right off the farm. Following a leisurely breakfast, they made three calls and called it a day. The second day they got up at 10 a.m., loafed through breakfast and made three more calls. Ditto the third day, but by now the young woman had to get back to Meridian and Tanner's mentor would have to drive her there. Lookee here kid, he said, be a good sport, make the rest of the calls yourself, turn in $200 or so of orders and tell the boss you had five days training.

The next day Tanner hit the road at 6 a.m. and by nightfall took in $1,000 worth of orders. Friday he got $700 more. It was so easy he couldn't believe it. When he got back to Memphis the manager didn't believe him until he checked out the orders himself and found out they were for real. The next week Berjon had a new sales manager in Mississippi.

When Tanner went to work for John Pepper at Pepper Sound Studios it was much the same. "He was a seven-day-a-week man, but I think he had a lot of fun too," said Pepper. "Bill is basically a salesman, and salesmen are always optimistic."

He would sleep in his car if necessary and work everyone under the table. There is a story that Franklin Roosevelt used to be able to draw a line across a map of the country and identify the counties and party chairmen in each state the line passed through. Tanner has something of the same talent. Name a one-horse town in the South and he can most likely tell you the call letters, owner and probably the ad rate of the local radio station.

Wilson Northcross, a business associate for nearly 25 years, said Tanner had an almost magical ability as a salesman. "One time we were down in Mississippi to do what they call detailing, where you went to a wholesaler and walked right back to the shelves to see which Berjon products they had," Northcross said. "We drove up to this place and as we walked past the counter the guy said 'Tanner, don't bother. I don't want any more of that stuff and furthermore I want you to get all your stuff back there out of here.' I'm thinking, good grief, how are we gonna make it? Well, with that introduction Bill walked out of there half an hour later replenishing the order. I never did understand how he did it."

Northcross continues, "He loved a confrontation. I think he looks on it almost like he looks on a sporting event. Really, I think Bill sees life like a competition."

The important thing about this period of his life was his introduction to barter, which he would later use to build his fortune. He was selling radio jingles and a deodorant called Everdry. Most of the little stations didn't have much cash so Tanner gave them the jingles for a little money and a chink of air time, which the stations probably couldn't sell anyway. (They was gettin' somethin' for nothin'. It was a great deal for them.") Then he would broker the air time to advertisers at a discount, often taking surplus goods in trade, which he swapped to other stations for still more time. Everyone thought they were getting a deal, but Tanner was getting the best deal. His second year he went cross country, and within three years he had opened up some 1,700 stations.

Tanner explodes with mirth as he recalls the countless times he got in the door by saying he was interested in buying some advertising, gassed up the owner by asking if he really believed his station could sell products and wound up getting his deodorant or whatever sold on a percentage of sales. "You heard Everdry comin' out your ears," he said.

The contracts with the broadcasters always contained a clause that said the air time or one-minute "spots" were "good until used." That might be a year from now, five years from now or even 15 years from now. By that time the station might be much more profitable and its spots selling for, say, $10 instead of $3. Some stations ran up quite a tab over the years and didn't always keep the best accounts. If the station was sold a couple of times, as many were, it could be a real mess. The new owner wouldn't know how much air time his predecessors had given away.

But Tanner knew, down to the minute. Over the years, more than a few cases wound up in court. A little radio station in Wisconsin balked at giving Tanner free time 12 years after the original agreement. The new owner had no records of the original contract and no idea how many unused spots there were. Tanner sued and won $14,723 for 2,778 spots at the then-going rate of $5.30. (When the time spots appreciated to $7.20 he filed an amended claim.) The granddaddy of these cases involved a Carolina broadcaster who owed 18,747 spots over 14 years. Tanner eventually collected $178,096.

Not all radio stations would trade with Tanner.

"My thinking was trading was of no value to me," said Robin

Mathis, owner of WCPC in Houston, Miss., for the last 30 years. "I thought it was the best discipline to pay cash. That way we'll always know what we owe each other."

In later years, Mathis got angry with Tanner's company when they would either pretend they had a barter arrangement or persist in trying to set one up. "The only way I could ever get it across to them," said Mathis, "was by telling them that if they ever mentioned barter to me or any of my people it would immediately negate our contract."

But enough stations bartered that after a few years Tanner had himself a time bank worth a couple million dollars on paper. He took it to a New York barter house which offered him 10 cents on the dollar. By his own account, he excused himself to go to the restroom and walked out the door. All of his efforts to work closely with or for someone else — the movie rentals, the Futurama Jet, now the time bank — had disappointed him. From now on he would make it or break it on his own hook.

"I always liked to do things my own way my own self. If it was gonna fail I wanted it to fail my way."

It was also during this period that Tanner learned to appreciate the salesman's gimmick of giving them something to remember you by. He gave boxes of candy, flowers, liquor, cars, jewelry. And "PMs" or "plush merchandise" incentives of a quarter or so on a $4 bottle of medicine to entice clerks to sell Berjon products.

The problem was he didn't know when to stop. He sees little difference in principle between "PMs" and the travel junkets some companies offer sales customers or the whole gray area of business favors. "I think most people would agree with me that that is the way business is done."

Giving money to people he probably should not have had nearly gotten Tanner in a jam before. For years he gave former Memphis State Athletic Director Billy 'Spook' Murphy $1,000 at Christmas "for a job well done." The ethics of doing this when Murphy was negotiating the Metro Conference's television package with the Tanner Sports Network seemed to escape him. Murphy, he reasoned, was "underpaid." His reputation as a soft touch got around when he became a rich man. He gave jobs to several worthy young men from Missouri and helped them go to Memphis State or get their start in business, but he also put several members of his family, including his sons, on the payroll. Forgetting the value of hard work he had learned back in Missouri, he spoiled his own children and bailed out some relatives and a few ne'er-do-wells.

"They all take advantage of him and he never said no," said Mrs. Riddick.

Meanwhile he was living lavishly. He made his first million at the age of 34. The Tanner Company expanded into travel, sports and overseas markets. Many of his personal luxuries, such as his Stutz Blackhawk with the gold-plated interior fixtures, came in barter deals. "I've never had anything that cost any cash," said Tanner, with only partial exaggeration. Not long ago, he admits, he was using rough, dispenser-variety paper towels at home because he had gotten them in a barter deal and didn't want to waste them. "It's not what you make — it's what you save," he said.

His third wife Pearline raised the kids. Tanner worked. His sister remembers him grief-stricken but still working even at his parents' funerals and at the hospital when his mother was dying.

The canny competitiveness that helped him get ahead in business carried over into his sports obsession, racquetball. About 10 years ago Tanner resolved to make himself an expert player. He hired David Bledsoe and David Fleetwood, two of the country's top pros, to play with him and give him lessons. Within a few years he was winning tournaments.

"He was probably the best in the country in his age division a few years ago," said Larry Liles, the coach of Memphis State's perennial national championship team and himself an excellent player. "He's probably one of the smartest players in the country. Every shot he makes he does with a purpose."

Even in practice matches Tanner follows a fixed routine. The game usually begins before the players take the court, with Tanner moaning good-naturedly about how poorly or infrequently he has been playing. Then he skips rope for a few minutes and goes off to a separate court to warm up. Once the game begins, Tanner doesn't give an inch.

"Some people call him a court crowder," said Liles. "He has been known to come off at some referees like (tennis player John)

McEnroe. I don't guess you could call him a clean player, but when the game gets close I don't know too many champions in any sport that you could call gentlemen."

Asked once if he ever took lessons from Liles, Tanner snapped, "Why would I do that? I beat Larry Liles." Liles, a much younger player, said that is not so.

Tanner promoted the sport and funded scholarships and new courts at Memphis State and Christian Brothers College during the mid-1970s. But for all his love of the game, he may have helped destroy its amateur arm, the International Racquetball Association. Its director, Luke St. Onge, had a falling out with Tanner, who had advanced the IRA some money to get started. When they split in 1977, Tanner sued for $14,000. The cash-poor organization was forced to settle out of court.

"The sport had enough problems," said St. Onge, now living in Colorado. "It was a time of real unsteadiness. A lot of people were vying for control. I'm just glad it's all behind."

The story illustrates two things about Tanner: First is his refusal to let sentiment get in the way of making a buck, even when the subject is as close to his heart as sports. "You've got to approach it like a businessman," he said. From time to time his name has come up in connection with this or that pro sports venture in Memphis. But he never got involved because he couldn't get the guarantees he wanted on the front end. When the football, soccer or basketball franchises eventually blew up, it was somebody else who got showered with red ink. The one sports venture he did sink his money into — Metro Conference basketball — proved to be a moneymaker for the Tanner Sports Network. Typically, he negotiated a 10-year contract when the league was new and hard up for exposure. Without it, "we probably would not have had any television," said Larry Albus, Metro Conference commissioner at the time. Tanner then stood firm when times got better and the league wanted to renegotiate with someone else. "They forgot their loyalty," he said.

"I always made sure I took care of Memphis State and the Metro Conference. Memphis was good for me. I think anyone who makes a living here should support the local colleges. That's something I think is wrong with a lot of people's thinking. They live here and make their living here but they went to Ole Miss and want to support Ole Miss, or they went to Tennessee and want to support Tennessee."

Secondly, the sue-the-bums policy was typical of Tanner and contributed to his public image, deserved or not, of being a bigshot who threw his weight around. A year after the scrap with the racquetball association, he spent $75,000 to fight a charge of assault and battery and resisting arrest in connection with a drunk-driving charge against his wife-to-be, the future Pat Tanner. (To this day he insists the arresting officer was abusive.) The day the well-publicized trial ended with the charges being dropped, the newspaper ran a big picture of Tanner and Pat, arm in arm, laughing as they walked out of the courthouse. They were celebrating but the picture made it look like they were laughing at justice.

In the minds of some people, nothing could offset such heavy-handedness, but Tanner tried. He gave generously and often to St. Jude's, the Memphis Arts Council and Memphis State. He turned his energy and talents to cancer drives and civic projects. He purchased what he said was $500,000 worth of Winston Churchill memorabilia and invited all the local social lions over to meet a Churchill relative for the unveiling. And he threw parties like his golf tournament blowout that were worthy of the Great Gatsby.

"This was all for the clients. It was never anything for me personally," said Tanner, a claim the IRS disputed. "We had to offset New York, Chicago and Los Angeles, the big cities."

Until two years ago he welcomed, even courted, publicity. Most rich men insulate themselves from reporters. Abe Plough rarely talked to them. Ron Terry prefers the company of editorial writers. Kemmons Wilson has a supply of funny stories and one-liners about his lack of formal education he regularly hauls out. Fred Smith has a squadron of flacks who politely tell the press he is out of the country. Tanner welcomed the calls of society reporters and was genuinely puzzled by the "one-sided, negative" publicity he feels began with the drunk-driving arrest. He keeps a scrapbook of all his newspaper clippings. In the 1960s and early 1970s a few reporters raised an eyebrow at the barter business, but far more typical was the columnist who wrote about Tanner's well-kept hair and his barbershop, featuring this breathless exchange:

"You know they're selling franchises, don't you," Bill asked.

"Gosh, no," I said.

It is not difficult to see why Tanner, gulping a 10-year diet of such pabulum, gagged on stronger stuff later on.

He cares about his public image but the suaveness of, say, a Fred Smith, has escaped him. Smith was Ivy League; Tanner is down home. Morley Safer fawned over Smith in a flattering piece on 60 Minutes; a reporter for Fortune magazine dined at Tanner's table then wrote that he served white wine with steak. It irked Tanner a little bit. For crying out loud, Smith started with money! But they did things differently too. Tanner flaunted his success in business and sports, in letters 10-feet high on his office building and on billboards (paid for by his own company) at the airports in Memphis and Nashville when he was named Tennessee's male amateur athlete of the year in 1981. But as you drive past the headquarters of Federal Express, there is not so much as a mailbox announcing that you are passing the office of one of the country's greatest business success stories of the last 20 years.

In a way Tanner's flamboyance is odd because, apart from the limelight and business contacts, he said he gets little genuine enjoyment from regular social obligations. He is too fitness-conscious to be much of a drinker and too shrewd to be impressed by snobs.

"You got a lot of flour-flushers. You got people who think partyin's everything. They think it will help you in business. It doesn't help you with business. To me it takes up your time, your money and ruins your health."

Reminded that he has been a prominent participant in Cotton Carnival and an organizer of Ptah, he said his wife Pat was a krewe queen one year and his ex-wife Pearline was a duchess.

"Probably at first I cared a lot," he admits. "I think a social image though is very bad for family and kids. I don't know if I spoiled them. I probably made it awful easy for them. I wanted them to have things I wasn't able to enjoy. They just got off on some drugs. I probably gave them too much money and cars. I was too liberal with them."

One-on-one he can be warm, funny and unpretentious. Posing for a picture in his study, he waves at a shelf of antiques and impressive looking ornaments and said, "I don't know anything about 'em, all I know is you're sposed to have 'em." Then he roars with laughter at his own joke.

He prefers a sweaty game of racquetball to golf or tennis, although he boasts that "I learn any sport after playing it twice." He can't stand the idleness of the country club lounge. Friends say his idea of a really fun night is a game of bridge or Trivial Pursuit and some ice cream.

The cocky, defiant face he showed the press and public at his news conference following the FBI raid in August, 1983, (complaining that the press treated him like "a cheap dope") wasn't there when he met with prosecutors over the next 17 months. Asst. U.S. Atty. Dan Clancy describes him as "pleasant." When he wasn't preoccupied with his legal problems (according to court documents he bugged offices at the William B. Tanner building, tapped telephones and ordered the destruction of files — a claim Tanner denies), Tanner immersed himself in work, running his United American Bank. He crowed that he was cutting into the business of the city's bigger, established banks. Ever the salesman, he revived a long-dormant banking process by giving away telephones to customers who opened new accounts. The bank's slogan: "Get some easy money."

He generally avoided self-pity in public. Around Christmas that year a friend came up to him and clapped him on the shoulder.

"Bill," he said, "they been kickin' you when you're down."

"That's OK," Tanner replied, "I got a big butt."

Privately, however, he felt the FBI was persecuting him. "They've got so many resources they can just keep coming at you," he complained. "They just wear you down." The day Jake Butcher was indicted he remarked that Butcher's guilt or innocence didn't matter. "They'll find something," he said glumly. When automaker John DeLorean announced after his cocaine trial that he was broke and seeking donations to offset his legal bills, Tanner said he was going to send him $100. He figured DeLorean was probably guilty but he sympathized with him.

Tanner would like people to believe that influenced his guilty plea, but Clancy scoffs at the notion as "absurd." The weight of the evidence against him is attested to by his four-year sentence, fines and income tax penalties that could easily exceed $1 million as well as the other guilty pleas attained with the help of his cooperation.

Tanner wanted to fight this one at first. It took sound advice from outside attorneys and the passage of time for him to come to understand he had done wrong.

"If I had realized, I would have talked to the attorneys more, got a professional opinion and listened to it. But it's hard when you're movin' fast and growin' and want to build the largest business in the world in that particular industry, make as much money as you can, you know. Sometimes you fail to stop, pause and realize what you're doin.' These are things that are very important. I think my attorneys probably told me but they didn't tell me strong enough. It takes someone strong to meet a strong moving force."

Could anyone really have told Bill Tanner how to run Bill Tanner's business?

"Probably that was one factor," he admits. "It's hard when you're successful, when you come from something that was nothing and build it to the largest in the world. It's hard to tell someone like that he was wrong."

When federal judge Robert McRae sentenced him to four years in prison, Tanner remained calm. "He probably took it better than (attorney James) Neal and I did," said attorney Cono Namorato. As the two were preparing to leave Memphis that day Tanner produced a gym bag. He tried to cheer them up with a little gallows humor, joking that he had brought his prison clothes and was ready to go. Then he thanked them, told them they had done their best and handed each of them a box. Inside each was a new pair of cowboy boots.

In a way William B. Tanner's story is so typical. Like thousands of Memphians he had come from the country with mud on his shoes, the smells of the farm still in his nostrils and a dream of a better life in his heart. He had a country name and a country accent. But he also had something else: a wonderful gift for selling and getting along with people and an overwhelming desire to make his mark. Had he grown up wearing shirts made of flour sacks? Then he would own 400 suits, 800 shirts, 100 pairs of cufflinks. Had he once sat on a wagon and driven a mule? Then he would drive the biggest, flashiest, most expensive car a man could buy, a match for the one owned by Elvis himself.

He would live in the biggest house, throw the biggest parties, rub shoulders with the biggest names. He would earn, and give away, money beyond the imagination of most people. He was so shrewd, so likable, so hard-working he didn't have to play outside the rules. He didn't have to cheat. So the toughest, most agonizing thing he has ever had to do was stand before a judge and say, yes, he did that too.

Working Stiff in
America's Distribution Center
(Memphis, 1998)

With its central location and headquarters of FedEx, Memphis is America's Distribution Center and boasts the busiest cargo airport in the world. The sprawling warehouses scattered around the city are a less glamorous part of the story. Representing dozens of companies, they employ over 100,000 Memphis-area residents. When a developer announces plans to build a new warehouse, it is usually treated in rah-rah fashion as an economic development story and then forgotten. To get the perspective from inside the box, I spent two works working in warehouses.

Working Stiff in North America's Distribution Center

" *One of the things (Wal-Mart founder) Sam Walton told me several times, sitting right in that chair where you are, is that retailing is about moving things. It's not about selling things.* "
— Federal Express founder Fred Smith

There are thousands of good jobs in North America's Distribution Center. This is not one of them.

I am packing cans of a spray cleaner called Office Duster at a warehouse on Presidents Island. It is 100 degrees outside but at least three degrees cooler inside where a fan that came over with de Soto pushes the hot air around. Delores, Bridget, and I are grabbing the purple cans off a conveyer belt and packing them 12 to a box. Some packaging fiend has contrived to attach a plastic straw to each can with a piece of tape. The straws make it easier to get to those hard-to-clean places in computers and office equipment. But they keep getting caught in the box dividers, slowing us down, and the purple cans are piling up on the overflow table and tumbling to the floor.

"That's good, that's the way, push them back down the line," Delores shouts at me by way of encouragement as I try to slow the advancing line of cans with my left arm while packing them with my right one.

My T-shirt and underwear are soaked with sweat, my back aches, and my legs are starting to cramp up. When I take five seconds to stretch, more cans go by and I fall further behind. As a temporary employee, I am making $5.75 an hour. Permanent employees like Delores and Bridget make $7 to $7.25 for packing. Bridget, who is half my size, is doing a third more work, and Delores, bless her, is catching the cans I miss, feeding me boxes, and cheering me on. We have temporarily outrun our supply train, filling boxes faster than the box-makers can stack them up for us. I make the rookie mistake of trying to pick up a full one from the conveyer line. The bottom falls out and 12 more cans crash to the floor.

After two hours of this, the line shuts down, the purple cans stop coming, and it is break time.

"Are they trying to kill us?" I ask Delores.

"This is nothing," she said. "You ought to work on aerosol," one of the other packing lines.

For two weeks I have been working eight hours a day in warehouses, getting a taste of what an estimated 40,000 Memphians do day and night, 52 weeks a year, year after year. I have made boxes, packed boxes, put little boxes into bigger boxes, slapped bar codes on boxes, loaded boxes on wooden pallets, and moved boxes around so that someone else can put them on a freight car, truck, or airplane or store them in some huge box of a building. The symbol of America's Distribution Center is not a jet or a computer chip or a barge. It is a box.

Memphis may be the box capital of America. All big cities have warehouses, of course. But Memphis has, as they say, the numbers: 5 million square feet of new space in one year, a location within a day's truck drive of 60 percent of the American buying public, and developers who can take an order for 600,000 square feet of space under one roof without blinking. It has know-how, flat land served by wide roads and cheap utilities, and the headquarters of FedEx.

And Memphis has one other vital ingredient: an abundant supply of unskilled labor willing to work as "casual" employees (meaning subject to termination on short notice), temporary employees (see above), seasonal employees, night workers, part-timers, and heavy-lifters.

If you trace a target over a map of the eastern United States, Memphis is the bullseye, hence the Chamber of Commerce began calling it America's Distribution Center in the 1970s. That has since been fine-tuned to North America's Distribution Center to encompass, among other things, the factories that have moved from the Rust Belt to low-wage Mexico.

The slogan and recruiting efforts that followed have been a smashing success. Nike, Disney, Starter, Sharp, Toshiba, and Williams-Sonoma are some of the companies with warehouse and distribution operations here. Even Silicon Valley comes to Memphis. Hewlett Packard is the latest of the marquee names moving into the yawning expanse of warehouse parks in southeast Shelby County.

Warehouses are a powerful if not glamorous engine of the red-hot Memphis economy. An estimated 100,000 people work at one of the more than 800 companies involved in some aspect of distribution. Or as USA Today put it in a jolly Christmas season front-page story last year, "96,000 elves get busy in Memphis."

The story didn't say whether all the elves would still be working come New Year's or how much they make each day in their various workshops.

No amount of jargon about technologistics can obscure the fact that product must be packaged and packages must be moved. At the bottom of the distribution pyramid is a large base of unskilled labor, teetering on the edge of poverty, jumping in and out of the work force, making $20,000 a year or less, and often patching together part-time jobs and $7-an-hour second jobs to make even that.

In some ways, the much-maligned Memphis City Schools system does a perfectly good job of supplying the labor for this market. The warehouse boom has occurred despite the lack of noticeable improvement in test scores and a dropout rate hovering around 30 percent. Most warehouse workers need not be neat in appearance, highly skilled, ambitious, or proficient in math or reading beyond elementary school level. One of the 47 warehouse help-wanted ads in a recent Sunday *Commercial Appeal* said "higher pay positions require the ability to read a ruler." You do not need to be handy with computers. You don't even need a diploma. The entrance exam is a drug test. You just need to be able to lift, move, and fill a box.

This is the world I wanted to see, from the perspective of inside the box. If only for a few weeks, I wanted to get as close to the experience of warehouse workers as possible. A friend offered to get me a job, but the search seemed to me to be part of the story. I used my real name and biographical information on applications but did not disclose my identity as a reporter. I wound up getting jobs through a staffing agency.

June 11th: I go to RPS, a trucking company, to fill out an application. They are advertising on the radio that they offer $9 to $9.50 an hour for package handlers on four shifts. The employment office is in a freight terminal at Mallory and Lauderdale next to the railroad yards. There are four other people inside when I get there. One applicant works nights at Kroger and is looking for a second job during the day. He looks worried about more than the heat and I soon see why. The interviewer asks him to pick up a 50-pound box and lift it to his chest, put it down, and do it again. He rubs his back, winces, and does it once. He's history.

"I haven't had one of those in a while," the interviewer tells me. I am the 470th person she has interviewed this week. She tells me I have to be able to handle 1,060 packages an hour. "It's hard but it can be done," she said. Let's see. Twenty packages a minute, a package every three seconds for five hours. Math skills like that and I can lift heavy boxes without getting a hernia, too. I'm scheduled for a second interview a week later. But I don't get the night job, because people with regular day jobs and college educations tend not to work out, the interviewer said.

This is the dilemma of night work. The RPS job is 20 hours a week. At $9.50 an hour, that's about $190 a week — good if you're a student or a second-wage earner, but barely $10,000 a year for a main breadwinner. There are some 560,000 jobs in Memphis. David Ciscel, a senior economics researcher and business professor at the University of Memphis, estimates that at least one in 10 Memphis workers have more than one of them.

June 15th: A staffing agency gets me a job at Global Household Products on Presidents Island. What you see is what you get on the island: steel fabricating, ironworks, chemical plants, trucks. The only restaurant, The Port, serves a massive sandwich called a barge burger and beer in a half-liter carafe. The main streets are named Harbor and Channel. The Disney warehouse in Hickory Hill where I later applied, on the other hand, is on Imagination Drive and employees are called cast members.

Workers at Global make and pack chlorine bleach products, rotating between rooms called the blue-line, drop-in, and X-14, which is the name of a mildew remover. I am packing a toilet bowl cleaner called 2000 Flushes. Pickers put 60 packages in a box, then I put three of those boxes into a bigger box and shove it through a machine that tapes it shut before it rolls down a conveyer belt to the pallet loader. The hamburger-sized tablets are made in the "dough boy room," so named because the workers in that room wear head-to-toe protective white suits that make them look like the puffy Pillsbury mascot. Chlorine will burn hands, face, and eyes, and several veteran employees have red marks to prove it.

My job is easy. The building is air-conditioned, and I adjust to the smell and dust so that I only need my breathing mask a few minutes at a time. I alternate between making boxes and loading boxes and slapping bar codes on them. I get two breaks and 30 minutes for lunch, and as a temp I make $8 an hour. Full-timers make $10 to $11 an hour. The line stops a lot because the green 2000 Flushes boxes keep getting jammed. By mid-afternoon I have packing boxes stacked all over the room.

The line stoppages give me a chance to talk to my fellow workers. Wanda is a divorced mother of two. She lives in Fayette County and commutes at least 45 minutes each way to work. She gets up at 4 a.m. to take the children to a relative's house and is sometimes not home until 6 p.m. The engine burned up on her car and she doesn't know how she will get to work for a while. "Hollywood" played minor-league baseball in the Dodger organization so long ago he remembers Roy Campanella. Sheila used to work in a bank but quit after it was robbed three times, the last time by a robber with an Uzi. Steve was laid off from a construction job. Nearly everyone said they have worked at one time or another at "the ramp" or the FedEx hub but prefer day work.

June 17th: Making boxes is not especially self-actualizing work. A reporter colleague suggests I will have lots of time to think when I'm away from the distractions of phones, newspapers, and memos, but the truth is I can't think of a damn thing of any consequence. My brain shuts down. The most profound thought I have is Studs Terkel's line that jobs aren't big enough for people. I try to take my mind off the clock by singing all the old beer commercials I can remember: Drewery's, Carling, Schlitz, Altes, Falstaff, Stroh's, Goebel, Hamm's. I go through my high school football and basketball teams for 10 years. I try singing spirituals — "Swing Low Sweet Chariot" seems to fit the rhythm of box-making. With the noise the conveyer makes, I can sing as loud as I please and nobody notices or cares. One-on-one I can talk to people, but when the jiving and trash talk starts I — the only white male in the room — am out of it.

Small kindnesses help, like passing someone a box, picking up product that falls to the floor, saying thank you and excuse me, folding the cardboard spacers so they go in the box easier. I find I will gladly do anything for anyone who calls me by name.

Management does what it can to make hard jobs bearable and treat employees with dignity. On my third day, there is a 45-minute meeting in the break room, complimentary donuts included. The plant manager talks about production goals. There are no condescending congratulatory banners or gimmicks. The manager wears a golf shirt and khakis, and his belly is creeping over his belt. Asked about absences, he shrugs and said he can count the number of days he has missed in years on one hand.

It isn't a pretty place, but how else is Mrs. America going to keep toilets and showers clean? At $8 an hour, I am making about half as much as my 13-year-old son who gets $25 for a two-hour lawn job. At the end of my week I smell like bleach but I sort of miss the place and mindless, honest work and the no-bullshit management. I'm clean-cut and a good worker. A couple of supervisors ask the temp agency what the deal is. They wonder if I'm in rehab.

June 22nd: My new job at W.M. Barr, a chemical company also on Presidents Island, doesn't pay as well. The building isn't air-conditioned. Temps make $5.75, full-time line workers start at $7, and go to $7.25 after three months.

I am assigned to working on the rust remover line. As cans are filled and labeled, I slap lids on them. Once I learn to slam the tops down with my palm like a machine instead of with my fingers, the job is easy. Pretty soon I'm holding five or six tops in one hand at a time while whamming them on with the other. After lunch, I figure I have done a few thousand or so.

Within a day or so, I learn that the place you don't want to be is "behind the wall." Behind the wall signs warn of organic solvents and halogenated solvents that can cause various dire consequences. There is an emergency shower. I am assigned to work with Jim, a big man in an apron and rubber gloves who mixes small batches of goopy black stuff that goes in quart cans. Jim said you paint it over blackboards. I am supposed to keep him supplied with cans and lids and clean up the cans if there are any drips, then box them up and load them on a pallet. But Jim almost never spills while filling 624 cans to a pallet, and I feel fairly useless.

Next to us, four other workers are packing boxes of urethane accelerator. Nita explains to me that it has to be contained in glass because it will burn through plastic. I ask if it will burn skin, too, and she gives me one of those looks adults reserve for small children who ask stupid questions. The packing process is labor intensive because the bottles are being shipped overseas. Each one has to be packed in Styrofoam, and boxed and sealed according to a seven-step process.

The plant has gone 422 days without a lost-time accident despite the temps like me, the forklifts running around, and all those organic and halogenated solvents brewing behind the wall. As someone who can't unload his dishwasher without breaking something once a month, I'm impressed.

June 24th: We are going to a different schedule tomorrow on account of the heat. Work will start at six in the morning instead of seven. Six of us temps are sitting in the break room. A guy named James is screwed. He takes the bus from downtown, and the first bus leaves at 6:20 a.m., so he can't work here.

Another temp had been making $12 an hour as a bricklayer on a church in Bartlett, but he couldn't take the 99-degree heat up on a scaffold all day. "Only the Mexicans can do it," he said. So he came here for half the money.

As bad as the job is, the break room isn't much better. It is air-conditioned but smells of microwaved bologna and Vienna sausages. In one corner, a television is tuned to a program called *Forgive and Forget*, which, because it is on television, naturally has everyone transfixed. Women tell sob stories to an Oprah look-alike, then walk across a room and open a door where they find either a forgiving friend or an empty space. A woman named Pam is telling the Oprah clone about the ring she stole from her best friend Barbara to get money for gambling. The camera switches back and forth between Pam and Barbara, who is watching a monitor in another room. I am pulling for Pam, but when she opens the door, Barbara isn't there. Pam nods in resignation. I walk outside to the dock and a blast of hot air to admire the architecture and high-grade industrial engineering of the Cargill corn-milling operation across the street.

A poster on a wall that reads "Give Us Your Sense" asks employees to suggest money-saving ideas. I am a walking example of one idea — a temp doing a low-paid job and glad to have it. I later learn that publicly owned staffing companies, once associated with the secretarial pool, are much more diverse. There are a score of them in Memphis, and they employ some 10,000 workers a day. Some of them are Wall Street favorites, and one executive, Mitchell Fromstein of Manpower, earned $4 million in 1996.

June 25th: Happiness is relative. So is job satisfaction. I worked six different jobs in my two weeks in warehouses. Someone within my eyesight always had a harder job than I did. In the dough-boy room, or behind the wall, or on the aerosol line it was always dustier, hotter, or the line moved faster. Or they had a story about a worse one on the scaffold, or in the spilled chemicals, or on the ramp. And someone else always had a better one filling the easy boxes, driving a forklift, working in air-conditioning, or making a few bucks more an hour. Or they had a story about a better one. On the one hand, this made the job you happened to be doing bearable. On the other hand, I could see how it could drive you crazy.

The day I applied for a part-time night job at $9 an hour, I came home and flipped on the television to see that auto workers at General Motors in Flint, Michigan, making nearly $40 an hour in wages and benefits, were on strike.

The U of M's Ciscel has been studying our economy since 1973. Many of his students work nights at FedEx. Mounted over his desk is a piece of paper with "The Four Ds of Manufacturing Employment: Dead-end Jobs, Dirty Jobs, Dark Working Environments, Dangerous Working Conditions." Sounds like warehouse work to me.

Every year he takes his MBA students to Mexico to see assembly plants where workers make $9 a day putting together the pieces that $20-an-hour workers in the stamping plants of the American Midwest made. In Mexico, employers proudly show their American visitor the shower stalls at the workplace. Big deal, Ciscel thought at first. Then it dawned on him that most workers don't have running water at home and a shower stall at work is a great perk.

"The break-even point for a real job in Memphis is about $10 an hour," he said. "You can survive and raise one child on $20,000."

Memphis is "a low-wage town, a semi-skilled town" that benefits from an influx of people from surrounding small towns where wages are even lower.

"The best jobs to come to the Memphis area in the last five years are in Tunica," where casinos employ some 15,000 people, Ciscel said. Other job growth areas besides warehousing and distribution include construction, where illegal aliens hold down wages; medical services, which is "cleaner but not high paid"; and restaurants and bars, which employ 32,000 people, many at minimum wage.

Business trends are likely to enhance Memphis' reputation as America's Distribution Center. From Wal-Mart to Dell Computer, pacesetter companies want the shortest possible time from the point of manufacture to the point of sale. But even the most sophisticated distribution systems still need one distribution point. And Memphis, for better and for worse, plays that role.

Shelby Foote and the
True Pulse of Life

(Memphis, 1996)

Shelby Foote

The Ken Burns PBS documentary The Civil War *made a celebrity out of Shelby Foote, who had the best stories, the deepest knowledge, the right accent, and a way with words. He had been interviewed numerous times about fiction, Mississippi, and the Civil War before I talked to him in 1996. So I focused on something he apparently had not talked much about for publication, namely Memphis, where he has lived for more than 50 years.*

Shelby Foote and the
True Pulse of Life

In an era of computers, grotesque celebrities, superficiality, and 180-page bestselling books about how to improve your love life or get rich, Shelby Foote is a refreshing throwback to another time.

He has written six novels and his 1.5-million-word, three-volume Civil War narrative in longhand with a dipped pen. In Ken Burns' 1990 PBS documentary, *The Civil War*, Foote honored both scholarship and the medium of television with his resonant voice, his insights, and his dignity. And when celebrity beckoned with opportunities to cash in, he did a most unusual thing. He looked it in the eye and turned his back.

His descriptions of the Civil War give readers and listeners, as Foote once wrote about the photographs of Mathew Brady, "a gritty sense of participation — of being in the presence of the uniformed and frock-coated men who fought the battles and did the thinking, such as it was."

He spent 20 years writing his Civil War series (the three volumes were published in 1958, 1963, and 1974, respectively), an achievement as remarkable as many of the great events he described. He has said he left out more good material than he was able to include. In the process, he gave away little of himself, taking as his model the ancient historians who believed that the actions and words of historical figures should speak for themselves. At the conclusion of Volume Two, however, he allowed himself one brief personal note. It speaks to the question a reader might have about the objectivity of a historian born and raised in Greenville, Mississippi, and currently living in Memphis:

"In a quite different sense, I am obligated also to the governors of my native state and the adjoining states of Arkansas and Alabama for helping to lessen my sectional bias by reproducing, in their actions during several of the years that went into the writing of this volume, much that was least admirable in the position my forebears occupied when they stood up to Lincoln."

The reference, of course, is to segregationists Ross Barnett, Orval Faubus, and George Wallace and their defiance of integration in the 1950s and 1960s.

Foote turned 80 this year but looks several years younger. Celebrity — "all this hoorah," he snorts — brings him loads of mail and frequent phone queries, most of them unwelcome. The problem is that he is pithy, gracious, and knows what he's talking about. All three qualities encourage the curious. In a face-to-face interview, he smiles and laughs a lot, like any good storyteller, and sends up a steady cloud of pipe smoke.

Novelist, Civil War historian, Southerner, Shelby Foote has been interviewed more than a few times. But he has rarely talked much about one other thing he most definitely is and has been for more than 40 years — a Memphian. Since 1953, he has lived in three parts of Memphis: the South Bluffs, where he wrote Volume One of *The Civil War*; East Memphis, where he wrote Volume Two; and his current residence, the old, high-ceilinged Tudor house behind a tangle of magnolia trees in Midtown, where he wrote Volume Three and now lives with his wife, Gwyn.

When I wrote to introduce myself and ask for an interview, he promptly replied by telephone that he would be glad to meet with me. We set up a time to meet at his house the following week. When I arrived at the front door, there was no answer, nor did anyone come to the back door when I knocked there. So I left a note with my card. He called me that night to apologize graciously for being out running an errand and to ask if he could please reschedule. I thought to myself, the author of *The Civil War* and the star of PBS owes *me* one? Of course I said yes.

In our interview, he seemed glad to not have to answer the same questions he had answered dozens of times. I started by asking him how he felt about Greenville, which has gained three casinos and lost much of its white population, writers including him, Walker Percy, and Hodding Carter Jr., and reputation as the Queen City of Mississippi in the last 50 years.

"I've only been to the casinos once," he said. "Made me want to cry. It's just terrible. I don't know what's going to become of all that. I regret very much the state being mixed up in it. I regret anybody being mixed up in it.

"I've had all kind of shocks to absorb in my life. One of the hardest I had is, I was raised up to believe that we in the Delta were sort of aristocratic and progressive and right-thinking in every way and the rest of the state was sort of benighted but we were the only thing that really mattered because of the richness of the soil and God knows. I came to find out that Tunica County was the poorest county in the United States. And it was a shock to me. It was so different from what I had been told. I'd also been told that all Negroes were happy from dawn to moonset. That wasn't true either."

Greenville, nearby Greenwood, and Memphis used to be the capitals of the Delta, places where women came to shop for shoes and designer clothes and planters marketed their cotton. Greenville's downtown business district has become a shell of what it was. Mount Holly, the antebellum Italianate mansion where Foote was born in 1916, is on Lake Washington, 15 minutes south of Greenville.

"It's a great shame, but there's a certain justice in it. The whole glory of the life that I lived up until I was 30 years old was based quite frankly on the exploitation of blacks. There was not a morsel of food in my mouth, not a shred of clothes on my back, not an hour of education that I ever had that didn't come out of exploiting some black somewhere or other. Either the servants in the house or the workers on the plantation that brought the money in. And then that was shut off when you couldn't get a cook for $3 a week. We had a woman named Nellie Lloyd who worked for us for 24 years. And she made $2 a week when she came to work and when she left she made $12 or $14 a week. It was all based on that kind of exploitation. It was as if it was designed by some group with a high, high rate of intelligence to trap the Negro into a situation and feel good about about trapping him."

When he was a boy, Beauvoir, the Jefferson Davis home in Biloxi, was a Confederate Veterans Home. The last Confederate veteran died in 1959.

"I've seen as many as 12 or 14 of them there," he said. "I didn't talk to any of them about the war and wouldn't have known what to ask them if I had. There's a story that really tickled me, and I'm sure it's true, too. They occasionally had receptions at these Confederate veterans places. These two women came to one and met this veteran who had lost his leg in the war, and they said, 'Oh my good man, you've lost your leg.' And he looked down and said, 'Damned if I haven't.'"

In the 1950s he moved to the South Bluffs area near where the Martyr's Park monument to victims of yellow fever now stands. The upscale houses that line the bluff were not built until the 1990s, and Foote was the only white person there when he moved in. He feared it would be raucous and violent, but it turned out to be "one of the quietest, mind-your-own-business places I ever lived." He would later use it as the main setting for his 1978 novel *September September*.

"Memphis had a wonderful past, and an iron curtain rang down," he said. "Mr. Crump rang it down. Mr. Crump never had a moral approach to government. He wasn't opposed to wickedness or being wicked. But when Prudential Life Insurance announced that Memphis was the murder capital of the United States, that's when Mr. Crump cracked down on the gamblers and whores and ran 'em out. And Memphis lost a considerable part of its soul when they ran those people out.

"He also did something else. The Memphis Police Department was truly brutal. He gave the cops almost unbridled license to do anything they wanted to keep violence down. When I lived on the bluff, there was an empty place next to me right where that 90-foot bluff is. I've seen the police bring people down there, and I've seen them standing out on the edge of that bluff, two cops and a suspect. I know exactly what they were telling him: We're going to throw you off this thing unless you admit that you did it.

"All the rowdiness of Memphis endears it to me. Even the injustices and everything else. Because it's got this true pulse of life to it. And that's what distresses me about television and so much of what goes on today. It doesn't have the true pulse of life to it. It's just an appeal to every phony aspect of our life."

He did not know Crump, who died in 1954, but talked to him once on the phone. He told Foote, "we bribe the people with good government." The infamous Lloyd T. Binford, guardian of Memphis morals for a quarter of a century as head of the Board of Censors, was still influential when Foote's first novels were published in the forties and fifties.

"About six months after I moved here, my fellow Legionnaires had a meeting to do something about all the smut that was coming into Memphis," he said. "They went to a bookstore down on Main Street and got three of my paperbacks, *Follow Me Down, Love in a Dry Season*, and something else, and took them to burn them. And on the way to the burning they said, 'Wait a minute, Hitler burned books, we shouldn't do that.' So they decided to throw them in the garbage dump instead."

Follow Me Down got a rare bad review from Paul Flowers, then the book editor of *The Commercial Appeal.*

"He said he was dismayed by it, and after he read it he felt like taking a bath in Lysol. I sent word to him, I wish you would take a bath in Lysol, full-strength."

Foote was a fan of the young Elvis Presley and his early recording of "That's All Right Mama." He called a friend of his agent to tell her about him.

"I told her there was a singer down in Memphis you all ought to get ahold of, his name is Elvis Presley. She said, 'Oh, we've got so many singers already we don't know what to do.'"

And he knew Henry Loeb, the two-term mayor of Memphis who was in charge of the city when Martin Luther King was assassinated in 1968.

"He got the least desirable job on the city council, which was garbage collection and that kind of thing, and he saw that it was done superbly. He'd get out himself early in the morning and ride around and see whether those people were doing their job, and he made a name for himself that way. Then all hell broke loose. And it was largely Henry's fault. Ned Cook (head of an international commodities firm) was his campaign manager. Right after he was elected I was talkin' to Ned, and I said, 'I hope you handle this Negro problem well, it is really important.' And Ned said, 'Let me tell you, there's nobody more appreciative of what the blacks have done and can do than we are. And believe me, anybody who comes to us with the right kind of attitude . . . Well, that about knocked me out. In other words, if he's got his hat in his hands we'll give him almost anything we can. Otherwise nothing. And that was a danger flag flying, right there."

He has been a friend of FedEx founder Frederick W. Smith for several years.

"Tunkie Saunders was a friend of both of us. Tunkie used to say his main ambition in life was to leave each of his children a million dollars. And I said I couldn't think of a worse thing to do than strap a million dollars on his back. That's awful. And he said, 'Well, look at Fred Smith, he couldn't have done a thing if he hadn't had the money to start out with.' And of course that's true. But I still believe it's a terrible thing to load a kid down with money. In *Citizen Kane*, Orson Welles said, 'Just think what I could have done if I hadn't had any money.' There's a lot of truth in that."

His writing output, once a regular 500-600 words a day, "has slacked way off on account of all this hoorah. I'll get back to it, and when I do it'll be just like it was before, I hope. I haven't got that many years left." His last published novel, *September September*, came out in 1978. The story of two Mississippi rednecks who kidnap a black boy contains some funny lines about Memphis such as "the three hardest dates in show business are Christmas, Easter, and Memphis" and "If God wanted to give the world an enema, Memphis is where he would insert the nozzle." There are also some funny sex scenes but without many four-letter words in them. I asked Foote if he would use a different vocabulary if he were writing fiction today.

"I don't think so," he said. "I wouldn't go for the four-letter-word thing. I never bridled back from them, I just don't think they're much use. I never thought they needed that. *The Red Badge of Courage*, I suppose, is still our best Civil War novel, and there is none of that in there. No need for it."

September September, later made into a movie with Memphis actress Cybill Shepherd, did not sell as well as Foote hoped it would.

"It's hard to know about that," he said. "Except for some very fortunate people, almost nobody can figure out what's going to be a bestseller. You can't do it that way. John Grisham has had runaway bestsellers, but I'm sure he didn't do it as a result of figuring out how to do it."

Foote's own reading choices are old-fashioned — Browning, Keats, and Proust, whose *Remembrance of Things Past* he has read from start to finish nine times.

"All art is built on previous art, always. And what looks like the wildest departure sometimes isn't a departure at all, it's just progress forward. I once told William Faulkner that I had every right to be a better writer than he was because his models were Joseph Conrad and Sherwood Anderson, and mine were Proust and him. And my writers were better than his writers He was kind enough not to point out the fact that there's another person involved there, namely the one doing the writing."

Like Faulkner, he has been asked to write screenplays but, unlike Faulkner, he refuses to do it. Movie director Stanley Kubrick wanted him to do a script about the Shenandoah Valley and the Civil War.

"I didn't want to get mixed up in that Hollywood business, all that golden weather and money and women," he said. "I figured that would be the end of me. So I was in New York and Faulkner was there and I told him I expect I better not get mixed up in that. He advised me to take the money and then get out. And he gave me a second piece of advice. 'Never take the work seriously but always take the people seriously because they can hurt you.' I took his advice but in reverse. I knew that I would take the work seriously and not pay any attention to the people, and I knew that I would get in trouble from that."

After more than an hour, I feared that I was imposing on him and wearing out my welcome. He had more than repaid me for missing our first appointment. I asked if he would care to come down to the South Bluff with me sometime and show me where his house used to be. My office is on the South Bluff and I often walk there. He sounded enthusiastic and said to call him.

When I did, though, I felt like one of those rude callers who want him to state the case for Nathan Bedford Forrest or confirm the number of casualties at Bull Run. The clipped voice on the phone said that he did not go to lunch but thanks just the same. It was a polite brush-off from a polite and private man whose offering to the public is his work, nothing more and nothing less.

Fred Smith
on FedEx and Memphis
(2004)

Fred Smith

Somewhere in the detritus of my desk I have saved a FedEx express letter from Frederick W. Smith that I hope my great-grandchildren will someday regard in the same light as a telegram from Samuel Morse or a phone call from Alexander Graham Bell. After a couple of interviews arranged by the Federal Express PR department fell through, I met Smith in 1986 through his friend Pepper Rodgers when they were near the start of their 10-year quest for professional football in Memphis. We played tennis regularly for several years after that, and I got a close look at the NFL chase, The Pyramid, the Flying Tigers acquisition, and the move into ground services.

Fred Smith
on FedEx and Memphis

F or Memphis, FedEx is the weight in the spider web, the pressure that can gently or not so gently change the shape of things as they are as well as things to come.

It employs 32,000 people in the metropolitan area, from box handlers working part-time at the Superhub at night to executives and pilots who own the million-dollar homes in the suburbs.

It pays health insurance and college tuition for thousands of Memphians who might otherwise be without either one. Its World Tech Headquarters boasts one of the brainiest and most cosmopolitan work forces in the South. When FedEx built a new suburban office complex and moved its headquarters, it created an instant boom in real estate prices, housing, and school construction. A payroll tax will never pass the Memphis City Council without its blessing. The Pyramid and FedEx Forum would not have been built without the support of its executives. Its jets make the noise Memphians hear in the middle of the night. In reruns of Seinfeld and the Tom Hanks movie *Cast Away*, FedEx is a Memphis icon in popular culture and entertainment.

For all that, Memphis can thank FedEx founder Frederick W. Smith.

Born in Marks, Mississippi, in 1944, Smith has been a Memphian since he was a small child. His father and namesake, a transportation industry mogul in his own right and founder of the Southeastern subsidiary of Greyhound Bus Lines, died of a heart attack when Fred was 4 years old. Fred grew up in Midtown on East Parkway South, moved out east as a teenager, listened to records with Ardent Studios founder John Fry, hung out at a Poplar Avenue drive-in called the Tropical Freeze, and attended Memphis University School with AutoZone founder J. R. "Pitt" Hyde III, graduating in 1962.

He has said that he "missed" the Sixties, or at least the Sixties in Memphis. After graduating from Yale, he joined the Marine Corps, completed a tour of duty in Vietnam as a platoon leader, then signed on for a second one as an aerial spotter. To this day, if he is hunting or out in the woods, he cannot look at a tree line without mentally figuring how to advance on it. He has said he did not expect to live to be 25 years old.

Happily for Memphis, he did. The FedEx story, or the Federal Express story as the company was known until the mid-Nineties, has become part of American business lore. It began operations in 1973 and now serves over 200 countries and has annual revenues of $25 billion.

With two of his Yale classmates, George W. Bush and John Kerry, running for president in 2004, Smith found himself fielding more than the usual number of calls from journalists and historians. He and Bush were in the same fraternity, although Bush is two years younger. He and Kerry were in the same class and senior club but were in different parts of Vietnam. Smith calls Al Gore "a close friend," and he has had more face time with Bill Clinton than most CEOs by virtue of the geographic proximity of Arkansas and Tennessee and lobbying for free trade, if nothing else. He is supporting Bush.

"I've given a lot of interviews about both Bush and Kerry, including Douglas Brinkley and his book *Tour of Duty*, and I finally just quit," said Smith, back home after taking part in the Memorial Day dedication of the World War II Memorial in Washington D. C., whose fund-raising committee he co-chaired with former U.S. Senator Robert Dole. "I couldn't afford the time. I'm kind of like the Forrest Gump of American politics."

The CEO of the state's second-largest corporate employer (to Wal-Mart) might be well advised to take the middle road in Tennessee politics. Memphis and Tennessee are two different political entities. Tennessee went for Bush over Gore in 2000, although Clinton won it in 1996, thanks to huge margins in inner-city Memphis. But East Memphis, where Smith's office is located, and suburban Shelby

County, where the company has relocated thousands of employees in the last ten years, are solidly Republican.

"I have felt for a long time that the pendulum in U.S. politics has swung back and forth way too far from the Roosevelt era of trying to be way too active to the sort of somnolent Fifties to the Great Society and the counter-reaction in the Reagan years," Smith said. "I don't think the country has found the balance necessary to go forward. The two political parties have probably been a good system for the United States, but I have the luxury of being an independent."

He is, of course, anything but a dim-bulb Forrest Gump. A better comparison might be to his friend and fellow Memphian Shelby Foote, the Civil War historian whose celebrity increased after his appearance in the 1990 PBS documentary by Ken Burns, *The Civil War.* Such a combination of insights, authority, adventure, and a southern accent is hard for interviewers to resist.

Among other things, Smith knows a lot about Memphis. He and his wife Diane have 10 children, giving him a parent's view of the ways the city has changed. He is a good tennis player with a court in his backyard. He keeps beer in the tennis house for his guests but rarely drinks one himself; he can swear like a Marine but doesn't and has been known to shout "crudburger!" when he gets mad. His regular partners are an eclectic group that includes only one other CEO, Allen Morgan Jr. He's a football fan who can watch his youngest son play for his high school on Friday night, another son play for the University of North Carolina on Saturday, and the Washington Redskins play in FedEx Field on Sundays. And he's a close follower of local political and business news and knows most of the players.

Why, then, did he start Federal Express in Memphis?

"To put a national hub-and-spokes system in place you have certain parameters that dictate where it can be. If you do a hypothetical box, it would start at about Memphis and go up to St. Louis and east to about Columbus, Ohio, and down to just east of Nashville. And you must put your hub in that location. If you look at the people who followed us, Airborne has a hub in Ohio, UPS has one in Kentucky, the Postal Service has one in Indiana. So the hub had to be in that box. The other criteria were weather, airport infrastructure, political support. We looked at Smyrna Airport in Nashville, we looked at Louisville, but when you put all those things together, Memphis came out on top."

The first night of operations is a matter of some disagreement, even in the company's own media materials. Smith recalls it as "pretty damn dismal."

"I learned that salesmen lie. I thought we were going to be buried in shipments. But we weren't. There were actually two start-up nights. The first one was so bad we actually took it down and went back to ground zero and started a month later. That's why you see two figures. It was only like eight packages the first night so we started a second time."

In 1977, the House and Senate approved the airline deregulation bill, clearing the way for Federal Express to become a giant in the air-express business and, not incidentally, for the future prosperity of unborn start-ups like Dell Computer that depend on just-in-time delivery. The staunchest opponent of the deregulation bill was Robert Prescott, the elderly founder and chairman of Flying Tigers. Prescott died in 1978. Years later, after Flying Tigers had been bought by Federal Express in 1989, his widow told Smith that he had confided to her at the time, "Those guys are going to beat us. They're tougher than we are." The respect was mutual. On Smith's orders, the first Flying Tigers 747 to be repainted with FedEx colors was christened "The Robert Prescott." But winning over the pilots of a rival company with a long tradition wasn't easy.

"When we looked at Flying Tigers, the key factor, as it is in all acquisitions, is to make sure there is a surviving or prevailing culture. The worst possible thing is to have an acquisition where cultures remain competitive with each other, such as Daimler Chrysler. At the end of the day, there must be one surviving corporate culture. It took longer on the pilot side because of difficult relationships, but they're as purple as anyone else today.

"In the case of our acquisitions of Caliber and Kinko's, we felt comfortable because their cultures were already similar to ours — very performance oriented, employee or customer-centered — so managing through those cultural issues was not without problems but it certainly was not insurmountable. We had to manage them, but we were pretty sure going in that we could do those things. If we weren't sure of those things, we simply wouldn't do a corporate development activity."

As a Memphis civic leader, Smith got personally involved in the construction of The Pyramid and the unsuccessful drive for a National Football League team.

"I think Memphis would have gotten an NFL team on the last go-round if it had been willing to build a new stadium. When St. Louis and Baltimore self-destructed, it created a great opportunity for Charlotte and Jacksonville. But I think the NFL would have preferred to have a city in the middle of the country in the Central Time Zone.

"As for The Pyramid, in its day it was successful for the Tigers and created some level of excitement downstream. The big problem now is that the remaining debt service should have been folded in with the debt service on the new FedEx Forum bonds, which is exactly what our CFO, Alan Graf, recommended.

"I think the NBA is the biggest thing that's happened around here in a long time. All you have to do is go to a Grizzlies game and look in the crowd and you see the top executives of every major corporation in town all over the place. I do think it has a real quality-of-life component for the corporate community."

Ten years ago, Smith was not optimistic about Memphis. It was difficult to recruit employees because of the lack of pro sports, the scarcity of big companies, and the dot-com bubble which gave people visions of quick money as consultants or officers with stock options.

"We addressed that by building the FedEx Technology Center in Collierville and our new world headquarters. With the opening of Bill Morris Parkway it is easy to get from there to downtown. People can live where they want to live. There have been some new private schools built which is very important. The new St. George's, the new Briarcrest, they are fabulous schools out there. People love working there. The quality of work life is much improved."

The FedEx work force in Memphis is more international and cosmopolitan than it was five or ten years ago. FedEx invested in technology centers at Christian Brothers University and the University of Memphis, where the vast majority of graduate degrees in math and science now go to either foreigners or first-generation immigrants.

"A high school graduate in Memphis could definitely go to either of those schools and enter a technical career at FedEx or another company. That wasn't the case ten years ago but it is today."

Employment now totals around 32,000 people in the greater Memphis area, adjusted for the offer of early retirement or voluntary severance that was accepted by more than 3,000 employees last year.

"I don't think employment in Memphis is going to decline and as the company gets bigger it will continue to drift up," Smith said. "The buyout offer hit its goals. You know, people know how to reach me through e-mail and so forth, and with the exception of a tiny number of people who changed their mind, I never heard one complaint, not one. It probably means we overpaid. That's fine. We tried to be generous and it's going to result in a cost savings of $235 million a year. And people are happy with it and it created a lot of opportunities for younger, more aggressive people to move up who were kind of stopped by the organization. Now growth has resumed in Express and International in particular is really going up."

The company has moved its headquarters away from Memphis International Airport as the commercial streets around the airport declined and the affluent population of Memphis moved east or into Shelby County or DeSoto County. Similar deterioration is happening in the Hickory Hill area adjoining the new world headquarters at Southwind. Several years ago, when Holiday Inns was still based in Memphis it moved its headquarters to what was then a greenspace on Lamar Avenue which rapidly declined.

"Memphis has got those issues in lots of different places," he said. "It's just a fact of life. You have to just have good security and hope for the best. Hopefully, the economic impact of our headquarters provides some sort of magnet for continued prosperity."

He believes the biggest challenge facing Memphis is getting its fiscal house in order.

"The level of debt is a very serious problem. We have spent ourselves into a hole. Whenever you pour money into a non-productive activity, whether you're talking about a corporation or a city with its educational system, you have a serious problem. The first thing they probably need to do is close some schools and stop building new ones where they don't have enough kids. It has been proven that that sort of politics does not work. If they do that, then I'm not pessimistic about Memphis. I think Memphis has a lot of attractions."

Southern Backwaters
and White Men in Suits
(2004)

What is news, and who says so? Daily newspapers and wire-services and the big-three television networks used to decide that, but that was before there were hundreds of cable television stations, the Internet, alternative newspapers, round-the-clock local newscasts, and Rush Limbaugh. Among the losers, at least in terms of news coverage, are the politicians and bureaucrats — white men in suits — who used to "make news" which other white men in suits presented, take it or leave it, to readers and viewers. Many left. Some of us are still trying to figure out how to get their attention.

Southern Backwaters
and White Men in Suits

As I have written elsewhere in this book, *Time* magazine called Memphis a "southern backwater" two weeks after the 1968 assassination of Dr. Martin Luther King Jr.

The label made some people in Memphis mad, but it stuck for quite a while because there was some truth to it. Certainly, I don't think most reporters like me who have spent much time in Memphis or Jackson, Mississippi would dispute it. Not only are those cities far removed from the great national news centers of New York, Washington, and Los Angeles, they were also just on the edge of the regional action. Arkansas had the Clintons and Whitewater. Nashville had Albert Gore and the NFL. In book after book and movie after movie and anniversary after anniversary, Memphis and Jackson and Ole Miss were tagged with their sordid past of assassinations and racial strife. I call it Mississippi porno.

My introduction to southern journalism came in 1979 from the United Press International Bureau in Jackson and a colleague named Billy James.

"Anybody got them chickens yet?" he would snarl each morning as another "Unipresser" or two wandered into the UPI office on the sixth floor of a downtown bank.

One of our daily duties was to provide our broadcast and newspaper clients with the Mississippi poultry and livestock reports. I forget whether someone had to make a phone call to get them or whether they came clacking over the wire, but I know we heard from our clients if they were not filed promptly. It required a certain amount of patience and perspective to stay with wire-service work if you were an ambitious young reporter in such circumstances.

I enjoyed working for UPI and thought it was excellent experience. You had to write thousands of words of copy every day, mostly rewritten newspaper stories for the broadcast clients, who demanded an 800-word news summary every hour. It taught you to use the short, declarative sentences that are the foundation of good journalism. In 1979, there were still five reporters in the UPI office in Jackson and five or six in the Associated Press (AP) office a couple of blocks away. Our primitive word processors were called tubes for some reason, and our stories went to the southern regional office in Atlanta for editing, then came back over the ticker. There was an A-wire or national wire, a regional wire, a message wire, and a weather wire. The machines spit out narrow roles of cream-colored paper that we ripped into sections and threw on the floor or hung on "the spike" for a day, and they made an unmistakable noise that is now a distant, pleasant memory.

There was competition between UPI and AP, which was called "Rox," in every bureau. Atlanta posted a little scorecard every morning showing how the papers in our coverage area had played each wire service's stories. A mini-scoop or an enterprising feature story might merit a 10-0 tally if the opposition failed to produce a "matcher" in timely fashion. It seems a little silly, but the competition and *esprit de corps* were healthy and produced better stories. Don't think for a minute that daily newspapers don't miss it now that most afternoon papers are gone. The surest way to get a story on the A-wire was to write about race or the Ku Klux Klan, whose members would sometimes muster a small rally in downtown Jackson. Another popular story produced by our office described the practice of "geophagy" or dirt-eating, which was supposedly practiced by the denizens of some rural county. These stories fit the preconceived notions that editors in New York had, and in my opinion still have in many cases, about Mississippi.

My worst trouncing was not really my fault but I remember it vividly. In Washington, a Mississippi congressman named Jon Hinson was arrested on a morals charge in a public bathroom. The AP had the news first, and it was all over the Capitol press corps in Jackson before UPI had a matcher. Reporters and red-faced, cherubic Rep. John Hampton Stennis, whose office was across the hall from the pressroom, were snickering and glancing furtively at me as I pecked away in ignorance on a story about some bill or committee meeting. Finally, Jim Young, the Jackson reporter for *The Commercial Appeal,* came over and tipped me off. I was the last one to know, and our clients were not happy.

Our bureau chief, Andy Reese, loved the Mississippi legislature and considered it by far our most important ongoing coverage when lawmakers were in session. By 1980, UPI was getting clobbered by AP in most markets, but we still had papers in Memphis, Greenville, Meridian, Tupelo, and Grenada and fed them a daily diet of legislative news. I call this period the heyday of white men in suits.

Until well into the 1980s, if a group of white men in suits met in a room in a state office building or a government building in Jackson or Nashville or Memphis and a wire service or newspaper reporter covered it, then chances are it was news. No matter how boring. Take it or leave it. White men in suits ran state government, City Hall, Cotton Carnival, Future Memphis, and the Chamber of Commerce. White men in suits met in a news meeting and decided what to put in the papers and in their editorials because, by God, some other white men in suits had held a meeting. Television stations took their cues from newspapers and wire services, and white men in suits on CBS, NBC, and ABC gave you the news.

Blacks and women got their say. White men in suits got their way. In 1982, a story about the Mississippi legislature contemplating a change in truck-weight limits from 72,000 pounds to 80,000 pounds could still make the front page of the two Memphis daily papers. You can look it up. I know because I wrote it, along with scores of others equally boring for the morning ("AMers") and afternoon ("PMers") papers in Mississippi and Memphis.

I have great respect for Capitol bureau reporters, but in my book the redefinition of news that is ongoing at *The Commercial Appeal* and other daily newspapers is justified and long overdue.

I left UPI in 1982, not long before it lost its clients in Greenville, Tupelo, and Meridian. It was sad leaving an organization that once boasted the likes of Merriman Smith, the famous reporter who, while fighting off the AP man, filed take after take of the shots fired at President Kennedy's motorcade in Dallas in 1963 and then ripped the phone out of the press car. My friend and UPI colleague Rheta Grimsley Johnson and I drove together to Memphis to interview at *The Commercial Appeal.* I got taken to lunch at the old Petroleum Club by the editor, Mike Grehl. Rheta got taken to the snack bar by the Tri-State editor. She was assigned to the Tupelo bureau, while I wound up on the Metro desk. But she got the last laugh because her feature stories earned her several awards and promotions, while I labored for a year on the graveyard and weekend shifts.

Unfortunately, Grehl became ill a few years later and never fully recovered. He was a reporter's editor, demanding and crusty and seen as standoffish by the Memphis establishment. He taught me to beware of any story that "walked through the door" or, in other words, was probably a PR piece, and to not write for my sources. Those are the two best pieces of advice I've ever heard about journalism. He was replaced by David Wayne Brown, a young guy who was put in the awkward position of being "executive editor" while Grehl's status was still uncertain. Brown went on to have a successful career in advertising with Conaway Brown. I enjoyed nothing but full support and good assignments from both Brown and Grehl and their successors, Lionel Linder and Henry Stokes.

The Commercial Appeal has been owned by the E.W. Scripps Company since 1936, and its forerunners were around for nearly 100 years before that. Whatever changes happen in a year or two, however drastic they may seem, should be looked at in that context. The trend is what matters. Old newspapers in Memphis and anywhere else look as dated as old cars and old clothes. They're all black and white and crammed with too many headlines and too much small type. The content of the front page and the other main news pages, I suggest, was defined too much for too long by what white men in suits did. Billy Graham's column still ran on the Metro page of *The CA* well into the 1980s.

For a long time, the money flowed from Memphis into the Scripps home office in Cincinnati as profitably and predictably as it now flows from Tunica casinos to Las Vegas. Maybe more. Documents found by the *Flyer* during a 1992 lawsuit showed that the *CA* was milking a profit margin of 36 percent in the late Eighties. Reporters like me were unaware of this and were lucky to get a merit raise of $25 or $50 above union scale. By design or not, it was a system that discouraged excellence.

Those days are over. Circulation that once topped 200,000 is now below 150,000 some days. Scripps gets 44 percent of its revenues from newspapers, down from 53 percent in 1998. Television and lifestyle channels like HGTV are the company's future. Several of my old colleagues have been put out to pasture.

Reporters do too much introspection. Most of the things that concern us greatly are boring "inside baseball" to people outside of our business. One of the only issues I can imagine possibly being of more general interest is the question of objectivity. I wrestle with it all the time. Is is better, I wonder, to get close to sources on a friendship basis or to keep things distant and strictly professional? And what about doing analysis and expressing opinions?

I've concluded it's better for me to have a few influential friends, especially if they're the type who respect your independence. And because I get my say-so only once a week, I often do analysis and express my opinions. After 20 years in Memphis I've earned pundit's rights. I want to be in philosopher Ludwig Wittgenstein's "stream of life," free to go where I want to go, see who I want to see, and say what I want to say and put my name on it. I hate the expression "naysayer" as a media putdown, and I think reporters who use it are pathetic toadies. Professionally, every good reporter has to be something of a naysayer. And it's absurd to suggest that someone who holds a job, owns a home, and raises a family in Memphis is not as civic-minded as the next person.

The worst part of this job, by far, is making an error, but it comes with the territory. Deliberate errors and fabrications, however, are something else. I have a touch of first-hand experience with plagiarism by a reporter for *The New York Times*, and I have criticized the local *Tri-State Defender* for stealing several stories from other publications. A community pretty much gets the newspapers it demands and deserves. I would give up just about anything before giving up my newspapers and would happily pay two or three times as much for them. I think *The New York Times, The Wall Street Journal,* and *The Washington Post's* web edition are among America's greatest inventions.

The *Memphis Flyer* came out in 1989 and I joined the paper and its sister publication *Memphis* magazine a year later at half a salary and the opportunity to freelance as much as I liked. If the rules of journalism were written in stone, the *Flyer, Nashville Scene, Arkansas Times* and other weekly alternative newspapers wouldn't exist. We should be the last ones to criticize change. It will take a couple more years to tell whether community journalism as now practiced in the *CA* and other dailies is a good thing or a bad thing. One key indicator will be whether they can attract and hold good reporters and news editors at the same time they're increasing coverage of pandas, pets, sports, and parties. If not, then it really will be a sad day because a monopoly daily newspaper is still a uniquely influential franchise, and there is no point in weekly newspapers pretending otherwise.

But until the shakedown period is over, ranting against community journalism is as hasty and pointless as ranting against the hundreds of offerings on cable television. The audience and advertisers rule. Daily papers and wire services and white men in suits lost their grip on the business a long time ago. Their view of the world and how that view should be presented is not now and never was, as one of their number, ex-Unipresser Walter Cronkite famously used to say, the way it is.

Credits

All photographs not taken by the author are used with permission.
The stories "Gordon Kahl's Ozark Odyssey," "William B. Tanner's Rise and Fall,"
"Dago: The Toughest Man in Memphis," and "Charles McVean, the Hackney Pony
Man" appeared in different versions in The Commercial Appeal and are used
with permission.

CPSIA information can be obtained at www.ICGtesting.com
Printed in the USA
LVOW12s1413200814

400089LV00001B/45/P